# Table of Contents

# Behold!

## I come like a thief

# Copyrights

Behold! *I come like a thief*
Title ID: 4599177
ISBN-13: 978-0-9890896-1-6
ISBN-10: 0989089614
Such a Time

Behold! *I come like a thief*

TO HIM WHO WAS, AND WHO IS,
AND WHO IS TO COME

# Introduction

This book focuses primarily on what has been referred to as the *rapture*. This Biblical event, whatever you choose to call it, has been misunderstood by many people. It has been overemphasized by some for the wrong reasons, and it has been underemphasized by others for lack of knowledge of its importance. This is a perfect example of how Bible scriptures can become twisted and distorted. There has been considerable confusion about this topic—for there are *pre-trib, post-trib, mid-trib, pre-wrath*, and *no-rapture* views of the *rapture*! But the view that is of most importance here is *not* any of the above, but rather, it is *God's view*.

The rapture-related scriptures are presented in a unique way in this book to make it enjoyable and easier for the reader to understand what Jesus was saying, but one must still invest the time to do the foundational reading. Doing so will give you the confidence and joy that only comes from experiencing God's word first hand.

I found that many things were not the way I had been taught. Perhaps you will feel the same. The confusion surrounding the *rapture* has created an atmosphere that has caused many Christians to feel uncomfortable, some to the point that they have avoided this topic completely. Many people find the Olivet Discourse, and especially the Book of Revelation, to be frightening and confusing. But remember, fear mostly comes from a lack of understanding. God does not

## Introduction

want us to fear, but to be bold instead. May God give us the eyes to see, the ears to hear, and the wisdom to perceive the truth of what he has to say to us in his written word.

## Chapter One

# Now and Then

The world is changing rapidly, more so today than I have seen throughout my entire lifetime, and it seems God is releasing more revelation into the hearts of believers every day. Although some things may not be crystalized in this present season, such as the seven thunders of Revelation 10:4, or the fifth-trumpet plague of locusts found in Revelation 9:1-12, God has his reasons for not giving us certain revelation until it is the proper time for us to know and to understand. But when the time is right, revelation must be released!

The Bible says, [1]"Blessed is the one who reads the words of this prophecy, and blessed are those who hear it and take to heart what is written in it, because the time is near."

Yet how can anyone take to heart something they haven't taken the time to understand? All they can really do is repeat what someone else has said, like political talking points. God doesn't want us to be parrots, but rather, to be diligent and to take the time to read his word for ourselves. We should also be asking him, "Father, what are you truly saying here?" It is so important that we personally approach God with our questions. For the Bible says, [2]"If any of you

---

[1] Revelation 1:3
[2] James 1:5

lacks wisdom, you should ask God, who gives generously to all without finding fault, and it will be given to you."

But realize that we also bring certain biases to the table that can influence the way we interpret God's word. Things we were taught or told as children, students, and adults, including things seen on TV, on computers, or at the movies, all have contributed to produce the concepts we believe today.

I have found that when I take the time to intensely meditate on God's word, those false images, ideas and misconceptions contained within me will often rise to the surface. Sometimes I don't recognize them at first. But if I keep focusing on what God's word has to say, that's when something amazing begins to happen: the mighty sword of the Spirit, which is the effective and powerful word of God, cuts through those intellectual strongholds, and cuts loose those blinders that try to rob me of true divine revelation.

When I feel pride or arrogance rise up within me, or when I begin feeling judgmental about someone who holds a different perspective than mine, it is often an indicator that what I am trying to protect is probably not really of God either. I have spoken with many people about their views of the end times, and I have come to realize that perhaps no two people believe alike. Therefore, it is important that we all focus on what God's word is really saying if we are ever to come together on these issues.

When I was in high school back in the early seventies, I was so excited about Bible prophecy. The late sixties had seen the shocking war between Israel and the surrounding nations. Hal Lindsay had just written his popular mega-seller book *The Late Great Planet Earth*, and things remained very active in Israel and elsewhere in the Middle-East.

My friends and I talked so much about end times. We thought things were so close to being fulfilled that Jesus could come at any moment to snatch us away in the *rapture*, and then the dreadful tribulation period would begin, that seventieth week of Daniel when the antichrist would reign over the entire world, and where the mark of the beast would be the symbol and catalyst of a global economic, political and religious system.

Many Bible teachers were teaching on end times, and Christian music groups were singing songs like, "*I Wish We'd All Been Ready,*" a song by Larry Norman about the *rapture*, where one person is taken and the other left behind. Sometimes when my Christian friends and I would say good-bye after talking about the end times we'd say, "Maranatha!"—an Aramaic expression meaning, "Our Lord comes," or "is coming," or else we'd say, "Here, there, or in the air!" and walk away with a smile.

Two summers ago I began sensing the Spirit of God directing me to revisit the end-times scriptures—to take closer look at the end-times prophecies of the Bible. My mission was clear; I was to daily seek God's wisdom, focusing solely on what the scriptures had to say. The scriptures alone would be my foundation, structure, and the primary influence of my thoughts. In doing so, I came to realize that many of the end-times concepts I had believed from my youth were simply myths—like worn, tattered hand-me-downs not fit to donate to any good cause.

I had been taught that all Bible prophecy had been fulfilled that needed to be fulfilled before Jesus returns for the gathering of his elect—and while we were away with Jesus, the world would be going through a terrible time of judgment called the Great Tribulation, a period of seven years of plagues, famines, pestilences, earthquakes, economic and political woes, accompanied by cosmic and cataclysmic events such that the world has never seen since mankind has inhabited this planet. Had God not shortened those days, no flesh would be saved.

I was taught that just as Noah's family was saved from the great flood, so also the Christians would be saved from having to go through the tribulation period. So, if you were saved from going to hell, then you were also saved from going through the Great Tribulation too. It was an incredible packaged deal for every Christian.

I must be honest, there *were* some scriptures that troubled me—scriptures that left me thinking that it might not necessarily *be* a slam dunk for every Christian. Scriptures like, [3]"Be always on the watch, and pray that you may be able to escape all that is about to happen, and that you may be able to stand before the Son of Man," or like, [4]"Therefore keep

---

[3] Luke 21:36 –Please note that all scriptures included in this book are quoted from the NIV unless otherwise noted.
[4] Matthew 24:42-44

14

watch, because you do not know on what day your Lord will come. But understand this: If the owner of the house had known at what time of night the thief was coming, he would have kept watch and would not have let his house be broken into. So you also must be ready, because the Son of Man will come at an hour when you do not expect him;" also like, [5]"Behold, I come like a thief! Blessed is he who stays awake and keeps his clothes with him, so that he may not go naked and be shamefully exposed."

These were scriptures that left me puzzled, and somewhat suspicious. How *do* we keep watch? How *do* we stay awake? What if we are caught up in the cares of this life at that very moment when he returns? What if we are not found waiting and watching—will we still be caught up, or will we have to go through the Great Tribulation? These types of scriptures left sobering questions in my mind. Although many believe to this day that the church is to be taken out before the Great Tribulation, and that it *is* a slam dunk, yet these scriptures, and others, still raise reasonable doubt in many minds.

Years have come and gone since the late sixties. I must admit, things look much more ominous all over the world today than they ever did in the late sixties and early seventies—and when I consider all the ways the US has changed since then, I just shake my head and pray God will have mercy on this nation. That, coupled with the news events

---

[5] Revelation 15:16

15

these days, has left many wondering about what lies ahead, and raises the question—how much longer do we *really* have?

Although I am convinced the scriptures clearly indicate that there are several prophesied events remaining that must be fulfilled prior to Jesus' return for his elect, it should not become an excuse for avoiding the subject, for time has a way of catching people off-guard.

The *rapture* is part of a very important event—an incredible event that we should *all* know more about, so when that day arrives, we will all be found prepared, expecting and waiting.

It's now time to take a closer look at what Jesus had to say, then afterward, we will consider what the prophets and apostles had to say as well. I was so amazed to find that what the prophets and apostles said was completely harmonious with what Jesus taught.  But why should anyone expect otherwise where God is involved?

## Chapter Two

# Merged Gospel Narrative
### *Olivet Discourse*

*(Matthew 24:1-51; Mark 13:1-3; Luke 21:5-36)*

While Jesus and his disciples were near the temple buildings one day in Jerusalem, his disciples asked him some questions that included, [6]"...what will be the sign of your coming, and of the end of the age?" He answered their questions with great detail.

The gospels of Matthew, Mark and Luke record what Jesus told his disciples up on the Temple Mount that day as they were marveling at all the magnificent buildings. These three gospel accounts also include what Jesus told Peter, James, John and Andrew a short time afterward while they were with him privately up on the Mount of Olives. Luke's gospel also records another related narrative by Jesus from an earlier occasion in Luke 17:22-35. On that occasion, Jesus was asked by the Pharisees about when the kingdom of God would come.

After responding to the Pharisees' question, Jesus then began sharing with his disciples privately about what things would be like in the days of the Son of Man—in the days preceding, and in the days following that time when his *sign*

---

[6] Matthew 24:3

would appear in the heavens. He shared with them that "...the Son of Man in his day will be like the lightning, which flashes and lights up the sky from one end to the other"—he was referring to that day when he will be revealed to the world.

Although there are other passages in the New Testament where his disciples share additional information regarding these end-time events, in this chapter we will focus primarily on what Jesus had to say about it from the gospel accounts of Matthew, Mark and Luke. John's Gospel is silent on this topic. When these three gospel accounts of Matthew, Mark and Luke are merged together contextually, we find that Jesus gave us a comprehensive picture of his comings.

So, in order to help us get the greatest impact, and the most complete picture of what Jesus was saying to us in these gospel accounts of Matthew, Mark and Luke about "the signs of his coming and of the end of the age," Jesus' words have been merged together into one narrative, a narrative based on the topical context of what Jesus said to his disciples that day.

In this *Merged Gospel Narrative*, the standard paragraph formatting has been removed, and new paragraphs have been established and numbered as parts 1 through 12. Each new paragraph has also been subtitled based on the subject context, but *none* **of Jesus' words have been changed, omitted or reorganized**.

It may seem a little redundant at times, but it is very important that nothing Jesus said be skipped while reading this *Merged Gospel Narrative.* For it is through this redundancy that Jesus' message and context can be most clearly and easily understood. Each gospel account appears in its entirety, but each passage has been interwoven with the others to form contextual thought paragraphs.

For your convenience, Jesus' entire narrative *without comments* may also be found in Appendix A, located at the back of this book, if you want to read it without the distraction of the added comments.

It is very important that you embed Jesus' teachings in your heart and mind so that it will be his voice you hear as you meditate on these things, and then compare what Jesus had to say with what his disciples also shared about the *rapture* in their letters found elsewhere in the New Testament.

# 1
# *The Temple Prophecies*
[Mt 24:1-2] [Mk 13:1-2] [Lk 21:5-6]

[Mt 24:1] Jesus left the temple and was walking away when his disciples came up to him to call his attention to its buildings. [Mk 13:1] As Jesus was leaving the temple, one of his disciples said to him, "Look, Teacher! What massive stones! What magnificent buildings!" [Lk 21:5] Some of his disciples were remarking about how the temple was adorned with beautiful stones and with gifts dedicated to God. But Jesus said, [Mt 24:2] "Do you see all these things?" he asked. "Truly I tell you, not one stone here will be left on another; every one will be thrown down." [Mk 13:2] "Do you see all these great buildings?" replied Jesus. "Not one stone here will be left on another; every one will be thrown down." [Lk 21:6] "As for what you see here, the time will come when not one stone will be left on another; every one of them will be thrown down."

### Comments

The disciples, so impressed by the magnificence of the temple buildings, call Jesus' attention to all the "magnificent buildings," the "massive stones," the "beautiful adornments," and the "gifts dedicated to God," perhaps thinking that Jesus would be as impressed by those things as *they* were—but instead, Jesus quickly refocused them from their pinnacle of excitement down to a more somber tone by prophesying to them, "As for what you see here, the time will come when not one stone will be left on another; every one of them will be thrown down."

What thoughts stirred inside the disciples' heads as Jesus prophesied the doom of their magnificent temple buildings? What were Peter, James, John and Andrew thinking as they followed Jesus down the Temple Mount, then up the Mount of Olives where they spoke with him privately? Were they thinking that the destruction of the temple Jesus had just prophesied about was somehow connected with the *end of the age*? Consider the type of questions the disciples asked him:

# 2
# *The Disciples' Four Questions*
[Mt 24:3] [Mk 13:3] [Lk 21:8]

[Mt 24:3] As Jesus was sitting on the Mount of Olives, the disciples came to him privately. "Tell us," they said, "when will this happen, and what will be the sign of your coming and of the end of the age?" [Mk 13:3] As Jesus was sitting on the Mount of Olives opposite the temple, Peter, James, John and Andrew asked him privately, [4] "Tell us, when will these things happen? And what will be the sign that they are all about to be fulfilled?" [Lk 21:8] "Teacher," they asked, "when will these things happen? And what will be the sign that they are about to take place?

## *Comments*

The disciples' questions to Jesus can essentially be consolidated to these four:

(1) When will these things happen? (the destruction of the temple buildings)
(2) What will be the sign that they [these things] are about to be fulfilled?
(3) What will be the sign of your coming?
(4) What will be the sign of the end of the age?

# 3
# *Beginning of Birth Pains*
### *[Mt 24:4-7] [Mk 13:5-8] [Lk21:8-11]*

**[Mt 24:4-7]** Jesus answered: "Watch out that no one deceives you. [5] For many will come in my name, claiming, 'I am the Messiah,' and will deceive many. [6] You will hear of wars and rumors of wars, but see to it that you are not alarmed. Such things must happen, but the end is still to come. [7] Nation will rise against nation, and kingdom against kingdom. There will be famines and earthquakes in various places. [8] All these are the beginning of birth pains." **[Mk 13:5-8]** Jesus said to them: "Watch out that no one deceives you. [6] Many will come in my name, claiming, 'I am he,' and will deceive many. [7] When you hear of wars and rumors of wars, do not be alarmed. Such things must happen, but the end is still to come. [8] Nation will rise against nation, and kingdom against kingdom. There will be earthquakes in various places, and famines. These are the beginning of birth pains." **[Lk21:8-11]** He replied: "Watch out that you are not deceived. For many will come in my name, claiming, 'I am he,' and, 'The time is near.' Do not follow them. [9] When you hear of wars and uprisings, do not be frightened. These things must happen first, but the end will not come right away." [10] Then he said to them: "Nation will rise against nation, and kingdom against kingdom. [11] There will be great earthquakes, famines and pestilences in various places, and fearful events and great signs from heaven."

### Comments

Notice that Jesus described this sequence of events as the "beginning of birth pains." This is the first of four end-times sequences that Jesus shared with them. These four sequences are parts 3 through 6 of this chapter, and they all collectively lead up to, and climax with, the *rapture* event. All four sequences may be found organized at the back of this book, in Appendix C, Sequences of Events, where each event has been numbered by order of occurrence.

Jesus' first sequence, part 3, the **Beginning of Birth Pains**, includes the following signs, summarized and in sequential order:

1. False messiahs appear and will deceive many.
2. Wars and rumors of wars.
3. Nation rising against nation, and kingdom against kingdom.
4. Earthquakes, famines and pestilences in various places.
5. Fearful events and great signs from heaven.

When the [7]false messiahs appear in the first event, item 1 above, they are *not* performing miracles, great signs or

---

[7] Matthew 24:5; Mark 13:6; Luke 21:8

wonders. This is very significant, because later on Jesus described another time when [8]"false messiahs and false prophets in that day will appear and will perform *signs and wonders* in order to deceive, if possible, even the *elect*." (See item 4, part 5, *Abomination that Causes Desolation*).

In other words, there will be one time when false prophets will appear and deceive many people using *natural* means; but there will be another time when false messiahs and prophets will appear, performing *signs and wonders* using *supernatural* means in order to deceive.

Societies all over the world are being prepared for this future time of great deception via the ever-increasing number of books, cartoons, board games, computer games, movies and TV series that include wizards, witches, magicians, magic spells, etc. Our younger generation has been totally prepped for such a time of supernatural powers and events.

After Jesus shared this first sequence of events with his disciples, he then diverted and addressed them directly, prophesying to them about the events that would personally influence their own lives.

---

[8] Mark 13:22

# 4
# *Personal Prophecies to the Disciples*
### Plight of the Early Church Jews
*"Before all this, they will seize you and persecute you."*
**[Mt 24:9-14] [Mk 13:9-13] [Lk 21:12-18]**

[Lk 21:12-18] *"But before all this,* they will seize you and persecute you. They will hand you over to synagogues and put you in prison, and you will be brought before kings and governors, and all on account of my name. [13] And so you will bear testimony to me. [14] But make up your mind not to worry beforehand how you will defend yourselves. [15] For I will give you words and wisdom that none of your adversaries will be able to resist or contradict. [16] You will be betrayed even by parents, brothers and sisters, relatives and friends, and they will put some of you to death. [17] Everyone will hate you because of me. [18] But not a hair of your head will perish. [19] Stand firm, and you will win life. [Mt 24:9-14] Then you will be handed over to be persecuted and put to death, and you will be hated by all nations because of me. [10] At that time many will turn away from the faith and will betray and hate each other, [11] and many false prophets will appear and deceive many people. [12] Because of the increase of wickedness, the love of most will grow cold, [13] but the one who stands firm to the end will be saved. [14] And this gospel of the kingdom will be preached in the whole world as a testimony to all nations, and then the end will come. [Mk 13:9-13] You must be on your guard. You will be handed over to the local councils and flogged in the synagogues. On account of me you will stand before governors and kings as witnesses to them. [10] And the gospel must first be preached to all nations. [11] Whenever you are arrested and brought to trial, do not worry beforehand about what to say. Just say whatever is given you at the time, for it is not you speaking, but the Holy Spirit. [12] Brother will betray brother to death, and a father his child. Children will rebel against their parents and have them put to death. [13] Everyone will hate you because of me, but the one who stands firm to the end will be saved."

## Comments

Notice that Luke's account has been positioned at the very beginning of part 4, instead of being arranged in the usual Matthew, Mark, and Luke arrangement. It was placed before Matthew's and Mark's accounts because Luke's account establishes the fact that the *Beginning of Birth Pains* events of part 3 are actually preceded by the **Personal Prophesies to the Disciples** events of part 4, listed next, so this summarized sequence actually occurs first, according to Jesus:

1. They will seize you and persecute you.
2. They will hand you over to synagogues and put you in prison.
3. You will be brought before kings and governors.
4. You will bear testimony to me.
5. I will give you words and wisdom that none of your adversaries will be able to resist or contradict.
6. You will be betrayed.
7. They will put some of you to death.
8. Everyone will hate you because of me.
9. Many will turn away from the faith and will betray and hate each other.
10. Many false prophets will appear and deceive many people.
11. The love of many grows cold as wickedness increases.
12. The Gospel will be preached to all nations.

Notice that in Matthew 24:14 and Mark 13:10 that both scriptures end with the fact that the gospel of the kingdom must first be proclaimed to all nations before the end will come. This began to be accomplished first by Jesus as part of his own ministry, and then afterward, it continued via the Great Commission, found in Matthew 28:16-20.

The Great Commission was a directive initiated by Jesus with his remaining eleven disciples that he had chosen, launching them from Jerusalem, to Judea, to Samaria, and outward into the world. Jesus commissioned them to "go and make disciples of all nations," and this charge is being carried out to this day by believing disciples across the globe, person to person, generation by generation, and although the end still hasn't arrived to this day, the end will come at its proper time—when the Father says it's time.

After Jesus had shared with his disciples those events associated with the *Beginning of Birth Pains*, and after prophesying to them about the things that would affect their own personal lives, he then advanced them to the next sequence, the *Abomination that causes Desolation* sequence of events.

# 5
# *Abomination that causes Desolation*
*"Then let those who are in Judea Flee to the mountains"*
*"There will be great distress in the land and wrath against this people"*
[Mt 24:15-28] [Mk 13:14-23] [Lk 21:20-24]

[Mt 24:15-28] "So when you see standing in the holy place 'the abomination that causes desolation,' spoken of through the prophet Daniel—let the reader understand— [16] then let those who are in Judea flee to the mountains. [17] Let no one on the housetop go down to take anything out of the house. [18] Let no one in the field go back to get their cloak. [19] How dreadful it will be in those days for pregnant women and nursing mothers! [20] Pray that your flight will not take place in winter or on the Sabbath. [21] For then there will be great distress, unequaled from the beginning of the world until now—and never to be equaled again.

[22] If those days had not been cut short, no one would survive, but for the sake of the elect those days will be shortened. [23] At that time if anyone says to you, 'Look, here is the Messiah!' or, 'There he is!' do not believe it. [24] For false messiahs and false prophets will appear and perform great signs and wonders to deceive, if possible, even the elect. [25] See, I have told you ahead of time. [26] So if anyone tells you, 'There he is, out in the wilderness,' do not go out; or, 'Here he is, in the inner rooms,' do not believe it. [27] For as lightning that comes from the east is visible even in the west, so will be the coming of the Son of Man. [28] Wherever there is a carcass, there the vultures will gather. [Mk 13:14-23] When you see 'the abomination that causes desolation' standing where it does not belong—let the reader understand—then let those who are in Judea flee to the mountains. [15] Let no one on the housetop go down or enter the house to take anything out. [16] Let no one in the field go back to get their cloak. [17] How dreadful it will be in those days for pregnant women and nursing mothers! [18] Pray that this will not take place in winter, [19] because those will be days of distress unequaled from the beginning, when God created the world, until now—and never to be equaled again. [20] If the Lord had not cut short those days, no one would survive. But for the sake of the elect, whom he has chosen, he has shortened them. [21] At that time if anyone says to you, 'Look,

here is the Messiah!' or, 'Look, there he is!' do not believe it. [22] For false messiahs and false prophets will appear and perform signs and wonders to deceive, if possible, even the elect. [23] So be on your guard; I have told you everything ahead of time. [Lk 21:20-24] When you see Jerusalem being surrounded by armies, you will know that its desolation is near. [21] Then let those who are in Judea flee to the mountains, let those in the city get out, and let those in the country not enter the city. [22] For this is the time of punishment in fulfillment of all that has been written. [23] How dreadful it will be in those days for pregnant women and nursing mothers! There will be great distress in the land and wrath against this people. [24] They will fall by the sword and will be taken as prisoners to all the nations. Jerusalem will be trampled on by the Gentiles until the times of the Gentiles are fulfilled."

## Comments

Jesus shared with his disciples another sequence of future events that, like the Personal Prophesies to His Disciples, would be a series of events that directly affect the lives of the Jews—but these are future Jews who will be living in Israel at the time when the actual *abomination that causes desolation*, referred to by Jesus, finally occurs. Following are the events of the **Abomination that Causes Desolation** sequence:

1. Jerusalem will be surrounded by armies just before its desolation is near. For this is the time of punishment in fulfillment of all that has been written.

2. The *abomination that causes desolation* will be seen standing in the holy place.

3. Then there will be great distress in the land and wrath against this [the Jewish] people.

4. "At that time...false messiahs and false prophets will *appear* and *perform great signs and wonders* to deceive..."

5. They [the Jews] will fall by the sword and will be taken as prisoners to all the nations.

6. Jerusalem will be trampled on by the Gentiles until the times of the Gentiles are fulfilled.

Jesus brings to his disciples' attention an event that, being Jews, they were probably very familiar with—that is, the "abomination that causes desolation spoken of by the prophet Daniel," an event that occurs at the midpoint of [9]Daniel's Seventieth Week. With the insertion of the parenthetical

---

[9] Daniel 9:20-27 (seven sevens, sixty-two sevens, and one seven, the one seven being Daniel's seventieth week of years when you add the number of sevens).

expression, "let the reader understand," found in Matthew 24:15 and Mark 13:4, it can be perceived that this *Abomination that Causes Desolation* event should be understood by those who will be alive and reading about this event in the future, when the time of its fulfillment approaches. However, many of the Jews believed back then, and many still believe today, that the *Abomination that Causes Desolation* prophecy was fulfilled when Antiochus IV reigned.

Some folks believe that it was Antiochus IV, King of Syria, who reigned from 175 B.C. and died in 164 B.C. who fulfilled this prophecy of Daniel. Antiochus IV also called himself *Epiphanies*, which means "illustrious," and according to [10]Jewishencyclopedia.com:

"He entered the Temple precincts, not out of curiosity, but to plunder the treasury, and carried away valuable utensils, such as the golden candlestick upon the altar and the showbread table, likewise of gold... An officer, Apollonius, was sent through the country with an armed troop, commissioned to slay and destroy. He first entered Jerusalem amicably; then suddenly turning upon the defenseless city, he murdered, plundered, and burnt through its length and breadth. The men were butchered, women and children sold

---

[10] http://jewishencyclopedia.com/articles/1589-antiochus-iv-epiphanes: *The unedited full-text of the 1906 Jewish Encyclopedia.*

into slavery, and in order to give permanence to the work of desolation, the walls and numerous houses were torn down...A royal decree proclaimed the abolition of the Jewish mode of worship; Sabbaths and festivals were not to be observed; circumcision was not to be performed; the sacred books were to be surrendered and the Jews were compelled to offer sacrifices to the idols that had been erected. The officers charged with carrying out these commands did so with great rigor; a veritable inquisition was established with monthly sessions for investigation. The possession of a sacred book or the performance of the rite of circumcision was punished with death. On Kislew (Nov.-Dec.) 25, 168 [B.C.], the "abomination of desolation" (שִׁקֻּץ מְשׁוֹמֵם, Dan. xi. 31, xii. 11) was set up on the altar of burnt offering in the Temple, and the Jews required to make obeisance to it. This was probably the Olympian Zeus, or Baal Shamem."

It is important to realize that the temple was *not* destroyed at the time of Antiochus IV; it was however looted, defiled and desecrated, but afterwards it was cleansed, purified and rededicated by the Jews.

That same temple was the Jerusalem temple that impressed Jesus' disciples so much—because King Herod, in no small effort to make a great name for himself, had undertaken a massive restoration campaign to restore and enhance the temple mount structures, enlarging and adding many features to the old temple buildings to make them look more impressive, creating memorials for himself. Herod also built many other fine buildings in his jurisdiction, including pagan temples.

The fact that Jesus is actually prophesying about the *abomination that causes desolation* as being a *future* event dispels the idea that the desecration of the Jewish temple under the reign of Antiochus IV is the fulfillment of the prophecy of Daniel, especially since what happened under Antiochus IV occurred back in 168 B.C., before Jesus was ever born!

Although it was indeed *an* abomination that caused another desolation of Jerusalem, it was not the *abomination that causes desolation* that Jesus was referring to. To better understand the timing of this passage as spoken by Jesus, one should carefully consider all things written in the Book of Daniel and elsewhere in the Bible concerning the *abomination that causes desolation,* while at the same time, one should also be considering those other events that are sequentially associated with it that must occur as well. In other words, we should be looking for the fulfillment of those other *related* events that the Bible says will precede *and* follow the *abomination that causes desolation.*

For example, In Daniel 9:25-27 there is a "covenant with many" that the "ruler who will come" will be part of, and he will be one who confirms or empowers that covenant with many. Daniel indicates that this seven-year covenant will mark the beginning of Daniel's seventieth week, and the *abomination that causes desolation* will occur at the half, or middle point, of that seventieth week, or exactly 1260 days after the covenant has been confirmed.

After the Anointed One (the messiah) is cut off, Daniel 9:26b says, "The people of the *ruler who will come* will destroy the city and the sanctuary. The end will come like a flood: War will continue until the end, and desolations have been decreed." Notice here that it is not the *ruler who will come* that destroys the City of Jerusalem and the temple, but rather, it is the people of the *ruler who will come* that do this—in other words, the *ruler who will come* will be from that same people group that destroys the City and the temple, but the *ruler who will come* cannot participate in the actual destruction of the City and the temple because he is a *future* ruler *who will come.* That is why the *ruler who will come* cannot be Titus, the Roman general in charge at the time. Remember, after Jerusalem and the temple are destroyed, this same passage says, "The end will come like a flood: War will continue until the end, and desolations have been decreed." Again, Jesus said war and *desolations* would be continuing till the end—not just one desolation, but desolations—plural.

The *abomination that causes desolation* will be the last desolation for Jerusalem—for it will be [11]"the time of punishment in fulfillment of all that has been written," according to Jesus. This final desolation will complete the

---

[11] Luke 21:22

prophecies concerning the desolations of Jerusalem as far as the *seventy sevens* that were prophesied by Daniel. Afterward, Jesus says Jerusalem will be trampled on by the Gentiles (non-Jews) until the time of the Gentiles has been completed.

It is very easy to confuse one event with another similar-sounding event that has already occurred in past history. For example, it is easy to assume that when the scripture says, "They [the Jews] will fall by the sword and will be taken as prisoners to all the nations," that this event already occurred back in 70 A.D. when Jerusalem and the temple were destroyed by a rebel faction of the Roman army led by the Roman General Titus. At that time, the Jews by necessity fled from the Romans, and tragically, those Jews who didn't escape were said to have been tortured, persecuted and killed, or forced to be Roman slaves.

Although the desolation of 70 A.D. was, without doubt, the fulfillment of Jesus' prophecy concerning the Jerusalem temple's destruction, where "one stone would not be left on another," it is important to realize that the *abomination that causes desolation* as described by Daniel, Jesus and the Apostle Paul, did *not* happen at that time. Also, since the *day of the Lord* events, as Jesus described them in orderly detail in his Olivet Discourse, did not occur, then the distress experienced by the Jewish people in 70 A.D. was not the great distress Jesus was referring to either.

Besides, if the *abomination that causes desolation* were to have actually occurred on a particular day in 70 A.D., then what covenant was it that was confirmed 1260 days *prior*? For the "Ruler who will come" was to have confirmed a covenant with many according to the Daniel Chapter 9 prophecy, in order for the *abomination that causes desolation* to occur in the middle of that seventieth week of Daniel.

Some think Nero was the one, but Nero *doesn't* qualify to be the *ruler who will come* either, for he did not do the things described in the Daniel 9:26-27 prophecy, nor do his actions conform to the *man of lawlessness* that the Apostle Paul described in his second letter to the Thessalonians, written about 51 A.D., where he clarified that the *day of the Lord* would be preceded by *the rebellion*, out of which the *man of lawlessness* would arise—Nero does not qualify as this individual for the same reasons Antiochus IV didn't qualify— because the *day of the Lord* didn't happen *immediately following* the distress of those days as Jesus prophesied in his Olivet Discourse.

So, neither Antiochus IV, Nero, nor Titus qualify to be the antichrist—the ruler who will come—the man of lawlessness—because none of these men, nor the events surrounding their actions related to the Jews and Jerusalem, even come close to fulfilling what the prophecies of the Bible literally specify will happen—Unlike the prophecies concerning the messiah, which were *literally* fulfilled regarding Jesus' first coming as the suffering Savior. Realize that about ten percent of the prophecies concerning the messiah were literally fulfilled on the very day Jesus was crucified, including many things which Jesus, the man, had no control over!

We really should be looking for prophetic events to be fulfilled literally, unless the scripture itself indicates otherwise. When God said that he was going to destroy the world by a flood, the world was *literally* destroyed by flood waters. It didn't mean a flood of evil, or something spiritualized that a flood might otherwise represent. Even prophetic "signs" are generally interpreted by the scriptures themselves, and the prophetic parables are most often explained or clarified by the scriptures either elsewhere in the Bible, or within the same passage.

In the second chapter of 2 Thessalonians, the Apostle Paul was very clear in explaining to the Thessalonians that the *day of the Lord* would not come [12]"until *the rebellion* occurs and the *man of lawlessness* is revealed," the one who "will oppose and will exalt himself over everything that is called God or is worshiped, so that he sets himself up in God's temple, proclaiming himself to be God." Please realize that just because a rebellion occurs, that doesn't mean it is THE rebellion referred to by Paul, or that the next lawless man to rise up out of a rebellion will be the antichrist. Paul is merely saying that before the *day of the Lord* comes, it will be preceded by *the rebellion*, out of which the *man of lawlessness* will arise, and afterward, the *day of the Lord* will eventually follow those events. **One must consider all the related events of a prophetic sequence in order to determine the authenticity of any particular event, for an authentic**

---

[12] 2 Thessalonians 2:3-4

event is best defined by the events that precede and follow it, when that event is prophesied as part of a sequence of events.

The sequential *"sign" events* presented by Jesus in his Olivet Discourse should not be ignored! In fact, the events of each of the end-time's related prophecies will all converge into an orderly sequence of events that will climax with the *rapture*, and then again with the *second coming* of the Lord to reign on the earth at the *end of the age*.

The "great distress upon this people" such as has never happened from creation until now, nor will again, and the dispersal of the Jews as prisoners to all the nations as spoken of by Jesus, these are events that will occur sometime AFTER the *Abomination that Causes Desolation*, but BEFORE the *day of the Lord* begins.

So if you may be thinking, as did the Thessalonians in Paul's day, that the *day of the Lord* has already occurred, then you may want to read the next sequence of events, *The Day of the Lord*, and consider *when* in all of recorded history did *these* events ever take place?

# 6
## *The Day of the Lord*
*"Immediately after the distress of those days"*
[Mt 24:29-31] [Mk 13:24-27] [Lk21:25-28]

[Mt 24:29-31] "Immediately after the distress of those days 'the sun will be darkened, and the moon will not give its light; the stars will fall from the sky, and the heavenly bodies will be shaken.' [30] Then will appear the sign of the Son of Man in heaven. And then all the peoples of the earth will mourn when they see the Son of Man coming on the clouds of heaven, with power and great glory. [31] And he will send his angels with a loud trumpet call, and they will gather his elect from the four winds, from one end of the heavens to the other. [Mk 13:24-27] But in those days, following that distress, 'the sun will be darkened, and the moon will not give its light; [25] the stars will fall from the sky, and the heavenly bodies will be shaken.' [26] At that time people will see the Son of Man coming in clouds with great power and glory. [27] And he will send his angels and gather his elect from the four winds, from the ends of the earth to the ends of the heavens. [Lk21:25-28] There will be signs in the sun, moon and stars. On the earth, nations will be in anguish and perplexity at the roaring and tossing of the sea. [26] People will faint from terror, apprehensive of what is coming on the world, for the heavenly bodies will be shaken. [27] At that time they will see the Son of Man coming in a cloud with power and great glory. [28] When these things begin to take place, stand up and lift up your heads, because your redemption is drawing near."

*Comments*

This sequence takes place [13]"immediately after the distress of those days." What distress is being spoken of here? It is the great distress upon the people of Judea that follows the *Abomination that Causes Desolation* event in part 5.

The **Day of the Lord** sequence includes the following events:

1. The sun will be darkened, and the moon will not give its light.
2. The stars will fall from the sky, and the heavenly bodies will be shaken.
3. Nations will be in anguish and perplexity at the roaring and tossing of the sea. People will faint from terror, apprehensive of what is coming on the world.
4. Then will appear the sign of the Son of Man in heaven.
5. All the peoples of the earth will mourn when they see the Son of Man coming on the clouds of heaven, with power and great glory.
6. He will send his angels with a loud trumpet call, and they will gather his elect from the four winds, from one end of the heavens to the other.

---

[13] Matthew 24:29

In response to their questions, Jesus shared with his disciples the many events or signs that would lead up to the destruction of the temple buildings, the signs preceding his coming, and the signs preceding the end of the age. He prophesied concerning his disciples personally, as well as concerning events effecting future Jews, and he does this all in four sequences of "sign" events. That doesn't mean these are the only *events* that will occur; it only means these specific "sign" events will occur in the order given by Jesus, and that we should be watching for these signs.

I have found that oftentimes sequences of events in the Bible are topical, and as such, they do not always include every single event that may occur between the first and the last event of the sequence, but instead, the sequence may only include those events that are specifically related to the topic of the sequence.

For example, let's say a person named Joe has lived in the following US states in the following order since his birth: Florida, California, Oklahoma and Texas. The topic of this sequence would be: *US states Joe has lived in since he was born*. However, what this particular sequence doesn't show is that between the time Joe lived in Oklahoma and Texas, Joe also lived oversees in Guatemala for five years. That doesn't mean that the sequence of *US states Joe has lived in since he was born* is incorrect, it simply ignores the fact that Joe lived in Guatemala because that information is not relative to the topic of the sequence.

Many sequences in the Book of Revelation are like this, and the end-times sequences of Jesus found in Matthew, Mark and Luke are somewhat this way—that is why the three gospel accounts have been merged together in this chapter, to provide the most complete picture of what Jesus was saying to his disciples.

# 7
## *Lesson of the Fig Tree & All Trees*
*"When you see these things happening,*
*you know that the kingdom of God is near"*
[Mt 24:32-35] [Mk 13:28-31] [Lk 21:29-33]

[Mt 24:32-35] "Now learn this lesson from the fig tree: As soon as its twigs get tender and its leaves come out, you know that summer is near. [33] Even so, when you see all these things, you know that it is near, right at the door. [34] Truly I tell you, this generation will certainly not pass away until all these things have happened. [35] Heaven and earth will pass away, but my words will never pass away. [Mk 13:28-31] Now learn this lesson from the fig tree: As soon as its twigs get tender and its leaves come out, you know that summer is near. [29] Even so, when you see these things happening, you know that it is near, right at the door. [30] Truly I tell you, this generation will certainly not pass away until all these things have happened. [31] Heaven and earth will pass away, but my words will never pass away. [Lk 21:29-33] He told them this parable:

43

'Look at the fig tree and all the trees. [30] When they sprout leaves, you can see for yourselves and know that summer is near. [31] Even so, when you see these things happening, you know that the kingdom of God is near. [32] Truly I tell you, this generation will certainly not pass away until all these things have happened. [33] Heaven and earth will pass away, but my words will never pass away.'"

### Comments

Luke's account makes it clear that the *Lesson of the Fig Tree and All Trees* is a *parable*. Moreover, Luke's account makes it very clear that this is not a parable about *just* a fig tree, but about *all* trees when their branches first become tender and begin to sprout leaves.

Therefore, this is *not* a parable about Israel, but rather, it is clearly a parable about the generation that observes the signs and events coming to pass that Jesus had just shared with his disciples. For just as leaves sprouting out on tender tree branches serve to indicate that summer is approaching, so likewise, when these *day of the Lord* signs suddenly start happening, these events will serve to indicate that the *Kingdom of God* is near.

Jesus says, "When you see *these* things happening, you know that *the kingdom of God is near.*" The parable then suggests that the term, "summer is near," represents the *kingdom of God* being near—*summer*, then, represents the *kingdom of God*. And so it will be that the generation that

44

observes the *day of the Lord* events coming to pass—*that* generation will certainly not pass away before the *kingdom of God* is given to God's faithful and wise servants to enjoy.

Jesus indeed gave his disciples a lot of information when he answered their questions up there on the Mount of Olives—and he answered their questions *completely*.

# 8
# *The Unknown Day and Hour*
*"Therefore keep watch, because you do not know*

*on what day your Lord will come"*
[Mt 24:36-44] [Mk 13:32-37] [Lk 17:22-37] [Lk 21:34-36]

[Mt 24:36-44] "But about that day or hour no one knows, not even the angels in heaven, nor the Son, but only the Father. [37] As it was in the days of Noah, so it will be at the coming of the Son of Man. [38] For in the days before the flood, people were eating and drinking, marrying and giving in marriage, up to the day Noah entered the ark; [39] and they knew nothing about what would happen until the flood came and took them all away. That is how it will be at the coming of the Son of Man. [40] Two men will be in the field; one will be taken and the other left. [41] Two women will be grinding with a hand mill; one will be taken and the other left. [42] Therefore keep watch, because you do not know on what day your Lord will come. [43] But understand this: If the owner of the house had known at what time of night the thief was coming, he would have kept watch and would not have let his house be broken into. [44] So you also must be ready, because the Son of Man will come at an hour when you do not expect him. [Mk 13:32-37] But about that day or hour no one knows, not even the angels in heaven, nor the Son, but only the Father. [33] Be on guard! Be alert! You do not know when that time will come. [34] It's like a man going away: He leaves his house and puts his servants in charge, each with their assigned task, and tells the one at the door to keep watch. [35] Therefore keep watch because you do not know when the owner of the house will come back—whether in the evening, or at midnight, or when the rooster crows, or at dawn. [36] If he comes suddenly, do not let him find you sleeping. [37] What I say to you, I say to everyone: 'Watch!' [Lk 21:34-36] Be careful, or your hearts will be weighed down with carousing, drunkenness and the anxieties of life, and that day will close on you suddenly like a trap. [35] For it will come on all those who live on the face of the whole earth. [36] Be always on the watch, and pray that you may be able to escape all that is about to happen, and that you may be able to stand before the Son of Man. [Lk 17:22-37] Then he said to his disciples, 'The time is coming when you will long to see one of the days of the Son of Man, but you will not see it. [23] Men will tell you, 'There he is!' or 'Here he is!' Do not go running off after them. [24] For the Son of Man in his day will be like the lightning, which flashes and lights up the sky from one end to the other. [25]But first he must suffer many things and be rejected by this generation. [26]Just as it was in the days of Noah, so also will it be in the days of the Son of Man. [27] People were eating, drinking, marrying and being given in marriage up to the day Noah entered the ark. Then the flood came and destroyed them all. [28] It was the same in the days of Lot. People were eating and drinking, buying and selling, planting and building. [29] But the day Lot left Sodom, fire and sulfur rained down from heaven and destroyed them all. [30] It will be just like this on the day the Son of Man is revealed. [31] On that day no one who is on the roof of his house, with his goods inside, should go down to get them. Likewise, no one in the field should go back for anything. [32] Remember Lot's wife! [33] Whoever tries to keep his life will lose it, and whoever loses his life will preserve it. [34] I tell you, on that night two people will be in one bed; one will be taken and the other left. [35] Two women will be grinding grain together; one will be taken and the other left. [37] 'Where, Lord?' they asked. He replied, 'Where there is a dead body, there the vultures will gather.'"

## Comments

Part 8, *The Unknown Day and Hour*, gives more specific details about the *rapture* event. Jesus informs believers what the world will be like at the time when the *Son of Man* is revealed, and Jesus explains what his servants *should* be doing at that time, when they first witness the events that precede the *rapture* beginning to unfold before their very own eyes—but he also informs his servants of the kinds of things they should *not* be found doing when he comes.

Jesus compares what the world will be like at that future day of his appearing, with what the world used to be like in past times just before God's judgment fell upon the wicked. For example, he reminded them what the world was like before the flood came and destroyed it, and he reminded them what Sodom and Gomorrah were like before fire and sulfur came down from heaven and destroyed those two wicked cities.

Jesus made it very clear that, just like past times of judgment, the wicked will be unaware of their impending doom, and he also reminded his disciples that the righteous, those who are aligned with God, and who follow God's instructions, will again be protected by a covenant—but the judgment will be swift and unexpected upon the wicked—for the end will come like a flood.

Notice that "The Unknown Day and Hour" narrative ends with Jesus saying in Matthew's account, [14]"If he comes suddenly, do not let him find you sleeping. What I say to you, I say to everyone: 'Watch!'"—We should take Jesus seriously, and be found watching and actively doing whatever he says we should be doing when we see the hour of his coming

---

[14] Matthew 24:36-37

quickly approaching. No, I am not saying that we should *look* busy at the last minute; I am saying we should live like there is not much time left.

Also, Jesus says something very important on the timing of his first return. The scriptures tell us, "[15]But about that day or hour no one knows, not even the angels in heaven, nor the Son, but only the Father."

So then, we can't know the *exact* day or hour when our Lord is coming. However, we *can* know when that day and hour are getting very close, because Jesus shared some of the signs to be looking for. He also told us what that day will look like so we'll be able to recognize that day when it finally arrives—even before the event of his coming actually happens; for there are certain events that will occur *on that day* just before the *rapture* takes place that same night. And although we can't know the exact hour of the night during which his coming will occur, we can know—within several hours of its actual occurrence—that the hour of his coming quickly approaches. How can we know this? Because Jesus says so himself! I know this sounds bold, but it's really true!

We must remember, though, when that day *does* come, one side of the earth will be night while the other side is day, and Jesus reminds us of this when he says, "two people will be in one bed; one will be taken and the other left. Two women will be grinding grain together; one will be taken and the other left." Yes, some people will be working, and some

---

[15] Matthew 24:36

will be asleep when that hour arrives. When it's daytime somewhere, it's evening elsewhere.

Also, we may want to consider Jerusalem time, because Jesus was speaking to Jews about these events. It may also be a good idea to know the time difference where you live compared to Jerusalem time.

So how do we know this will occur at night in Jerusalem? Because Jesus said so in Luke 17:30-35, where he shared, "It will be just like this on the day the Son of Man is revealed...On that night, two people will be in one bed; one will be taken and the other left. Two women will be grinding grain together; one will be taken and the other left." This indicates that it will be a global event—some people will be working while some people will be sleeping.

But, you ask, just how do we know it will take place during one of the four watches of the night? It is because Jerusalem nighttime consisted of four watches, from 6:00 p.m. to 6:00 a.m. These four watches of the night in Jerusalem were:

(1) First Watch: *Evening,* 6:00 p.m. to 9:00 p.m.

(2) Second Watch: *Midnight,* 9:00 p.m. to 12:00 a.m.

(3) Third Watch: *Cockcrow,* 12:00 a.m. to 3:00 a.m.

(4) Fourth Watch: *Morning,* 3:00 a.m. to 6:00 a.m.

Also, because in Mark 13:32-37, Jesus said this:

"But about that day or hour no one knows, not even the angels in heaven, nor the Son, but only the

Father. Be on guard! Be alert! You do not know when that time will come. It's like a man going away: He leaves his house and puts his servants in charge, each with their assigned task, and tells the one at the door to keep watch. Therefore keep watch because you do not know when the owner of the house will come back—whether *in the evening, or at midnight, or when the rooster crows,* or *at dawn.* If he comes suddenly, do not let him find you sleeping. What I say to you, I say to everyone: 'Watch!'"

What Jesus was showing us here in Luke 17:30-35 was that "On the day the Son of Man is revealed," it will be "on that night" that the "one will be taken and the other left behind" event will take place—yes, the *rapture!* But it will be "on that night" *Jerusalem time.* What time will that be where you live? It could still be daytime where you are, perhaps.

Realize that the *Day of the Lord* events that precede the *rapture* will be globally observable events, judging by Jesus' description of them. This also means that when the *day of the Lord* actually begins, if you know what time it is *in Jerusalem,* and then calculate the number of hours until the first watch of that night occurs, then from *that* time, sometime within the next twelve hours, and within one of those four watches of the night, the *rapture* will indeed take place. For if Jesus said it will happen "on that night," then it will have to occur during one of the watches of the night.

However, we still do not know exactly *which* hour that will be, and we won't know either—until it happens! Of course, we could get more technical about this and say that it can't happen during the twelfth hour, because if the *rapture* doesn't occur within eleven hours of the four watches of the night, then there is only one hour left, so it would *have* to be *that* one—but then, we would know beforehand which hour that would be, and that would not work, because Jesus said no man knows the hour! Did you follow that? If not, don't worry about it—it won't matter.

But the *rapture* will occur during one of those watches, Jerusalem time, and in the Mark 13:32-37 passage, Jesus also confirms this with a clear message to those who serve him— that the Master's return will take place during one of the four watches of the night!

The context of Jesus' warning in Mark 13:24-31 is clearly linked to the time when the Son of Man returns "in clouds with great power and glory," when he sends his angels to "gather his elect from the four winds, from the ends of the earth to the ends of the heavens," and that the *rapture* event follows the *day of the Lord* events. The *day of the Lord* events will be discussed in more detail later on, so just keep these things in mind.

It is at this point that the gospel accounts of Mark and Luke leave off from the Olivet Discourse of part 8, and only Matthew's account alone continues to complete the Olivet Discourse, parts 9 through 12.

Parts 9 through 11 contain the following themes:

(9) The faithful, responsible servant vs. the irresponsible hypocrite—*Faithful and Wise Servant Parable*, Part 9;

(10) Preparation for oneself vs. expectation of entitlement from others—*Ten Virgins Parable*, Part 10;

(11) Good stewardship and reward vs. laziness and punishment—*Bags of Gold Parable*, Part 11.

Finally, in part 12 of this chapter, Jesus returns to Earth, but this time, it is "When the Son of Man comes in his glory, and all the angels with him." It is the time when "he will sit on his glorious throne." Part 12, then, completes Jesus' answer to his disciples' questions about the signs of his coming, and of the end of the age, as Jesus concludes with sharing about the Kingdom Age, found in Matthew 25:31-46.

There will be no further comments following parts 9 through 12 of this chapter.

# 9
## *Faithful and Wise Servant Parable*
### [Mt 24:45-51]

"Who then is the faithful and wise servant, whom the master has put in charge of the servants in his household to give them their food at the proper time? [46] It will be good for that servant whose master finds him doing so when he returns. [47] Truly I tell you, he will put him in charge of all his possessions. [48] But suppose that servant is wicked and says to himself, 'My master is staying away a long time,' [49] and he then begins to beat his fellow servants and to eat and drink with drunkards. [50] The master of that servant will come on a day when he does not expect him and at an hour he is not aware of. [51] He will cut him to pieces and assign him a place with the hypocrites, where there will be weeping and gnashing of teeth."

# 10
## *Ten Virgins Parable*
### [Mt 25:1-13]

"At that time the kingdom of heaven will be like ten virgins who took their lamps and went out to meet the bridegroom. [2] Five of them were foolish and five were wise. [3] The foolish ones took their lamps but did not take any oil with them. [4] The wise ones, however, took oil in jars along with their lamps. [5] The bridegroom was a long time in coming, and they all became drowsy and fell asleep. [6] At midnight the cry rang out: 'Here's the bridegroom! Come out to meet him!' [7] Then all the virgins woke up and trimmed their lamps. [8] The foolish ones said to the wise, 'Give us some of your oil; our lamps are going out.' [9] 'No,' they replied, 'there may not be enough for both us and you. Instead, go to those who sell oil and buy some for yourselves.' [10] But while they were on their way to buy the oil, the bridegroom arrived. The virgins who were ready went in with him to the wedding banquet. And the door was shut. [11] Later the others also came. 'Lord, Lord,' they said, 'open the door for us!' [12] But he replied, 'Truly I tell you, I don't know you.' [13] Therefore keep watch, because you do not know the day or the hour."

# 11
## *Bags of Gold Parable*
### *[Mt 25:14-18; 25:19-21, 22-23, 24-30]*

[Mt 25:14-18] "Again, it will be like a man going on a journey, who called his servants and entrusted his wealth to them. [15] To one he gave five bags of gold, to another two bags, and to another one bag, each according to his ability. Then he went on his journey. [16] The man who had received five bags of gold went at once and put his money to work and gained five bags more. [17] So also, the one with two bags of gold gained two more. [18] But the man who had received one bag went off, dug a hole in the ground and hid his master's money.

[Mt 25:19-21] After a long time the master of those servants returned and settled accounts with them. [20] The man who had received five bags of gold brought the other five. 'Master,' he said, 'you entrusted me with five bags of gold. See, I have gained five more.' [21] His master replied, 'Well done, good and faithful servant! You have been faithful with a few things; I will put you in charge of many things. Come and share your master's happiness!' **[Mt 25:22-23]** The man with two bags of gold also came. 'Master,' he said, 'you entrusted me with two bags of gold; see, I have gained two more.' [23] "His master replied, 'Well done, good and faithful servant! You have been faithful with a few things; I will put you in charge of many things. Come and share your master's happiness!'

[Mt 25:24-30] Then the man who had received one bag of gold came. 'Master,' he said, 'I knew that you are a hard man, harvesting where you have not sown and gathering where you have not scattered seed. [25] So I was afraid and went out and hid your gold in the ground. See, here is what belongs to you.' [26] His master replied, 'You wicked, lazy servant! So you knew that I harvest where I have not sown and gather where I have not scattered seed? [27] Well then, you should have put my money on deposit with the bankers, so that when I returned I would have received it back with interest. [28] So take the bag of gold from him and give it to the one who has ten bags. [29] For whoever has will be given more, and they will have an abundance. Whoever does not have, even what they have will be taken from them. [30] And throw that worthless servant outside, into the darkness, where there will be weeping and gnashing of teeth.'"

# 12
## Sheep and Goats Parable
### [Mt 25:31-46]

[Mt 25:31-40] "When the Son of Man comes in his glory, and all the angels with him, he will sit on his glorious throne. [32] All the nations will be gathered before him, and he will separate the people one from another as a shepherd separates the sheep from the goats. [33] He will put the sheep on his right and the goats on his left. [34] Then the King will say to those on his right, 'Come, you who are blessed by my Father; take your inheritance, the kingdom prepared for you since the creation of the world. [35] For I was hungry and you gave me something to eat, I was thirsty and you gave me something to drink, I was a stranger and you invited me in, [36] I needed clothes and you clothed me, I was sick and you looked after me, I was in prison and you came to visit me.' [37] Then the righteous will answer him, 'Lord, when did we see you hungry and feed you, or thirsty and give you something to drink? [38] When did we see you a stranger and invite you in, or needing clothes and clothe you? [39] When did we see you sick or in prison and go to visit you?' [40] The King will reply, 'Truly I tell you, whatever you did for one of the least of these brothers and sisters of mine, you did for me.'"

[Mt 25:41-46] Then he will say to those on his left, 'Depart from me, you who are cursed, into the eternal fire prepared for the devil and his angels. [42] For I was hungry and you gave me nothing to eat, I was thirsty and you gave me nothing to drink, [43] I was a stranger and you did not invite me in, I needed clothes and you did not clothe me, I was sick and in prison and you did not look after me.' [44] They also will answer, 'Lord, when did we see you hungry or thirsty or a stranger or needing clothes or sick or in prison, and did not help you?' [45] He will reply, 'Truly I tell you, whatever you did not do for one of the least of these, you did not do for me.' [46] Then they will go away to eternal punishment, but the righteous to eternal life."

# Chapter Three
# The Rapture &
# Day of Redemption

The word *rapture* is not found in the popular English translations of the Bible. The term *rapture* is believed to have originated from the Latin [16]Vulgate. It comes from a Latin translation of the Greek word *Harpazo* that comes from a Greek New Testament phrase that, according to the Thayer & Smith Greek Lexicon, means "to claim for one's self eagerly, and to snatch out or away," and which has often been translated as [17]*caught up* in the popular English translations of the Bible.

Jesus taught his disciples about the timing of this great event, and he even gave it a name—he called it their "redemption." Be careful not to jump to conclusions here thinking that Jesus was talking about the redemption of their spirits and souls. He's wasn't. He was talking about the

---

[16] The first Vulgate (A.D. 400) was the standard Latin version of the Bible, the translation of which is usually attributed to Jerome. Jerome was a scholar who was commissioned by Pope Damasus I to translate a version of the Bible that would become the standard Latin text in order to promote universal doctrine in the Catholic Church. Prior to the work of Jerome, there were many varied texts in circulation causing confusion within the church. There have been three versions of the Vulgate: the Clementine Vulgate, the Stuttgart Vulgate, and the Neo-Vulgate (*Nova Vulgata*). The Neo-Volgate has been the current official text of the Catholic Church since 1979.

[17] Thayer and Smith. "Greek Lexicon entry for Harpazo." "The NAS New Testament Greek Lexicon". . 1999.

redemption and transformation of their physical bodies, an event which hasn't happened yet, even to this day. If you think it has, then maybe you should to take a closer look in the mirror—if you're still enamored with what you see, good for you. But for the rest of us still living in these body *tents*, it certainly will be something to look forward to.

The phrase translated *caught up* is found in 1 Thessalonians 4:16-18: "For the Lord himself will come down from heaven, with a loud command, with the voice of the archangel and with the trumpet call of God, and the dead in Christ will rise first. After that, we who are still alive and are left will be *caught up* together with them in the clouds to meet the Lord in the air. And so we will be with the Lord forever."

Many English words have Latin roots. Such is the case with the *rapture*. All three versions of the Latin Vulgate use the term *rapiemur* to translate the Greek word *harpazo*. *Rapiemur* has *rapio* as its root Latin verb, and it means [18]to seize, snatch, tear away; to plunder a place; to hurry along a person or thing; 'se rapere', [to rush off]. Transf., [to pervert, lead astray]. N. of partic. as subst. raptum -i, [plunder].

Since the Latin root verb *does* conceptually have the same meaning as the Greek word *harpazo*, then the theological use of the term *rapture* for describing this *caught up* event would seem to be a more accurate translation than

---

*caught up*, except that only a few of the English dictionaries have actually added this theological meaning to their definitions for the term *rapture*. Regardless of whether you choose to use *rapture,* or use the Biblical expression *caught up* instead, it is still important to remember the actual meaning of the word *harpazo* that was used in the Greek manuscript in order to understand the real nature of this event.

What you call it is really not so important, because the *rapture*, or "caught up" event, is only one part of a multifaceted gem of an event—that event being *God's miraculous redemption of the body of fallen man.*

This is the [19]*redemption* event spoken of in Romans 8:22-23, where Paul says, "We know that the whole creation has been groaning as in the pains of childbirth right up to the present time. Not only so, but we ourselves, who have the firstfruits of the Spirit, groan inwardly as we wait eagerly for our adoption to sonship, the *redemption* of our bodies."

In Ephesians 4:30, the Apostle Paul also says, "...do not grieve the Holy Spirit of God, with whom you were sealed for the *day of redemption.*"

It is this same *redemption* that Jesus spoke of to his disciples while up on the Mount of Olives, for he explained to them that: "There will be signs in the sun, moon and stars. On the earth, nations will be in anguish and perplexity at the roaring and tossing of the sea. Men will faint from terror, apprehensive of what is coming on the world, for the heavenly

---

[19] Greek word, "Apolutrosis," Strongs No. 629

bodies will be shaken. At that time they will see the Son of Man coming in a cloud with power and great glory. When these things begin to take place, stand up and lift up your heads, because your *redemption* is drawing near."

Although Jesus was soon to redeem the spirits and souls of his disciples via his suffering and death on the cross, their redemption would not be complete, for they would still have to wait for the *redemption* of their bodies. That is why when we die to this day, our spirits and souls go to Heaven to be with the Lord, but our bodies remain on this earth awaiting the resurrection promised by Jesus at the *last day*. So, until then, he [20]gave his disciples, and he gives us, the Holy Spirit as a guarantee to strengthen our "earthly tent" until that day when God will clothe us with our "eternal house."

Remember, Jesus said to his disciples, [21]"Do not let your hearts be troubled. Trust in God; trust also in me. In my Father's house are many rooms; if it were not so, I would have told you. I am going there to prepare a place for you. And if I go and prepare a place for you, I will come back and take you to be with me that you also may be where I am."

This future *day of redemption* will be the day when our redemption is complete, for "When Christ who is our life shall appear, then shall we also appear with him in glory." We will finally be what God intended: a redeemed spirit and soul contained within a redeemed immortal, physical body.

---

[20] 2 Corinthians 5:1-5
[21] John 14:1-3

## Redemption Transformation

It all happens on the night when the Lord comes like a thief to snatch away those who belong to him; and he will clothe them with imperishable, glorified bodies because he's bringing them back with him to Heaven. Our existing bodies could not survive such a rapid trip from Earth to Heaven. The Apostle Paul says it like this: "I declare to you, brothers, that flesh and blood cannot inherit the kingdom of God, nor does the perishable inherit the imperishable. Listen, I tell you a mystery: We will not all sleep, but we will all be changed—in a flash, in the twinkling of an eye, at the last trumpet. For the trumpet will sound, the dead will be raised imperishable, and we will be changed. For the perishable must clothe itself with the imperishable and the mortal with immortality. When the perishable has been clothed with the imperishable, and the mortal with immortality, then the saying that is written will come true: "Death has been swallowed up in victory." "Where, O death, is your victory? Where, O death, is your sting?"

## Day of Redemption

The *day of redemption* begins with the Lord himself descending from Heaven, and it ends with the Lord returning to heaven with his fully-redeemed elect. Therefore, just to clarify things, we are speaking about those who are in Christ, but who have fallen asleep in death before the Lord returns; and their spirits and souls are with Jesus now in Heaven, but their dead bodies remain on the earth in some state of decay or as dust. Remember that for the believer, to be [22]absent from the body is to be present with the Lord, according to the Apostle Paul. Therefore, if a believer's body is dead, and his remains are still on the earth, then only his or her spirit and soul are present with the Lord in heaven.

Jesus will be [23]bringing the spirits and souls of the redeemed who have died and gone to Heaven back with him to Earth when he descends from Heaven into Earth's atmosphere in order to complete his *redemption* process. He will do this by resurrecting their dead bodies, gathering and transforming them from their deteriorated, corrupted physical state into an incorruptible, immortal, and glorified physical state like his own [24]glorified body that he received after he himself was resurrected and transformed.  Paul said, [25]"...Christ has indeed been raised from the dead, the firstfruits of those who have fallen asleep;" and he also said in Philippians 3:20-21, "But our citizenship is in heaven.  And we eagerly await a Savior from there, the Lord Jesus Christ, who, by the power that enables him to bring everything under his control, will transform our lowly bodies so that they will be like his glorious body."

Once those in Christ who have fallen asleep in death have been resurrected, then those of us who are still alive at his coming will also be transformed and gathered to meet the

---

[22] 2 Corinthians 5:1-10
[23] 1 Thessalonians 4:14
[24] Phillipians 3:20-21
[25] 1 Corinthians 15:20

Lord in the atmosphere. Afterward, the angels will transport all those who have been fully redeemed up to Heaven, along with Jesus, to be with the Lord forever. When will this take place? Jesus said in Matthew 24:29-31: "Immediately after the distress of those days" 'the sun will be darkened, and the moon will not give its light; the stars will fall from the sky, and the heavenly bodies will be shaken.'" "Then will appear the sign of the Son of Man in heaven. And then all the peoples of the earth will mourn when they see the Son of Man coming on the clouds of heaven, with power and great glory. And he will send his angels with a loud trumpet call, and they will gather his elect from the four winds, from one end of the heavens to the other." Jesus also said in Luke 17:24, "For the Son of Man in his day will be like the lightning, which flashes and lights up the sky from one end to the other."

**Signs of His Coming**

Jesus says there is coming a time when [26]"there will be signs in the sun, moon and stars. On the earth, nations will be in anguish and perplexity at the roaring and tossing of the sea. Men will faint from terror, apprehensive of what is coming on the world, for the heavenly bodies will be shaken." So as the world is stressing over these things, the sun and moon will suddenly darken. The stars will fall from the sky, and on that day, the celestial lights of our solar system will be suddenly darkened by God, like a theater when its house lights are

---

[26] Luke 21:25-26

dimmed, just before the main show is about to begin. And it is during this time of darkness, that the world's attention will be redirected upward into the heavens, like a spotlight, as the sign of the Son of Man appears resplendent, like lightning that flashes and lights up the sky from one end to the other. The whole world will take notice, and the peoples of the earth will mourn when they see the Son of Man coming on the clouds of heaven, with power and with great glory.

From Paul's third letter that was written while he was imprisoned in Rome, he wrote: [27]"When Christ, who is your life, appears, then you also will appear with him in glory."

So we see that the *day of redemption,* which includes the *rapture,* is actually a rapid and orderly sequence of events resulting in the physical transformation of the dead and living bodies of those who are in Christ, changing their natural bodies into glorified bodies like the one Jesus received after his resurrection. Remember, Jesus could still eat, drink and be touched, unlike a ghost or a spirit.

In fact, the Bible says, in 1 Corinthians 15:20, that "...Christ has indeed been raised from the dead," and that he was "the first-fruits of those who have fallen asleep." This means that Jesus' body was the first to be transformed into an incorruptible, immortal, glorified body. All those before him who had been raised from the dead were returned to their mortal, corruptible bodies, only to finish out their lives and to eventually die again.

---

[27] Colossians 3:4

## Kingdom of Our Lord and of His Christ

The *day of redemption* will certainly be an exciting day for many—but it will be a dreadful day indeed for most people on this planet still living under the tyranny of the antichrist. But did you know that the *rapture*, or the *last day*, is also the last day of man's official reign on the earth? It is man's last day because it is the day when the [28]"kingdom of the world becomes the kingdom of our Lord and of his Christ." Revelation 11:15-18 shows us that it is immediately AFTER the seventh trumpet of Revelation has sounded that God then takes his authority and begins his reign from Heaven over the kingdom of the earth—just before his wrath is poured out on the earth below.

## The First Gathering

Now, some people are confused about whether Jesus will be coming back only once, or if he will actually be making two trips back to the earth. According to the scriptures, he will be coming back twice—first, as we have already discussed, to gather his elect by extracting them from the earth, those who have already died, and those who are still living, transforming them both, and then gathering them all up into the earth's atmosphere, where Jesus will have already descended from heaven to meet them; then the angels will transport those gathered to the other end of the heavens.

---

[28] Revelation 11:15 (The seventh trumpet)

## The Second Gathering

Later, as the *time of wrath* ends, our Lord returns to the earth again, but this time he comes back to execute judgment over his enemies at the Battle of Armageddon, at which time the false prophet and the antichrist will be thrown alive into the Lake of Fire, the wicked armies that have amassed to make war against him will be destroyed, and he will send his angels out for the second gathering: to gather and to separate those who are still living on the earth after the *time of wrath*, as a shepherd separates the sheep from the goats, punishing the goats, and then rewarding the sheep by giving them their Kingdom inheritance. This *second-coming* event by the Lord is referred to as the *Harvest* and it occurs at the *End of the Age.*

Let's now summarize: The [29]*rapture (last day)* occurs at the sounding of the *last trumpet* of Revelation following the [30]*Day of the Lord* events. The [31]*time of wrath (Bowl Judgments)* occurs after the *rapture,* after the seventh and last trumpet of Revelation has sounded, and after "the kingdom of this world has become the kingdom of our Lord, and of his Christ"—but Jesus remains in heaven during this time with the Father, and [32]with his *elect,* while the angels administer the wrath of God at the Father's command, when the Father alone occupies the heavenly temple. For John, in his vision, saw the

---

[29] 1 Corinthians 15:51-54; 1 Thessalonians 4:13-18
[30] Luke 21:22-28; Mark 13:24-27; Matthew 24:29-31
[31] Revelation 16:1-21
[32] 1 Thessalonians 4:17b

heavenly temple [33]"filled with smoke from the glory of God and from his power, and no one could enter the temple until the seven plagues of the seven angels were completed!"

The *time of wrath* commences when the bowl judgments commence, and it ends when the seventh bowl has finally been poured out, and when the Father [34]declares from his throne in the heavenly temple, "It is done!"

The [35]*End of the Age (Harvest)* occurs after the *time of wrath*. It is the time when the Lord returns to Earth with the host of heaven, and with his elect, and he [36]destroys the antichrist, the false prophet, and the massive international army gathered at Armageddon to wage war against him at his arrival, and then he [37]reigns for a thousand years in the *Kingdom Age* while [38]Satan is bound in the Abyss.

The *end of the age* is also a transitional time—from age to age—for it is the end of one age, and it is the beginning of a new age—the *Kingdom Age*. [39]"The kingdom of the world *has become* the kingdom of our Lord, and of his Christ."

To be clear, the *rapture* is the caught-up or gathering part of the *day of redemption* that occurs once the bodies of those who are in Christ have been transformed into immortal bodies. This *day of redemption* event occurs at the *last day,*

---

[33] Revelation 15:8
[34] Revelation 16:17
[35] Joel 3:13; Matthew 13:30; 13:39;25:31-33;Revelation 14:15-16
[36] Revelation 19:11-21;20:1-3
[37] Revelation 20:4-6
[38] Revelation 20:2
[39] Revelation 11:15

but the *Harvest* is a different event completely, and it occurs after the *time of wrath*, at the *End of the Age*—two separate events—and they occur at different times.

However, since the *rapture* is an integral part of the events that collectively are referred to by Jesus and the Apostle Paul as *the redemption*, and since most people are already familiar with the term *rapture*, then, for this book, we will expand its meaning when using the term *rapture* henceforth to include all of the sub-events associated with that glorious *day of redemption*:

## Sub-events Associated with the *Redemption*

1. The *day of the Lord* events (sun, moon & stars) occurring first, followed by the sign of the Son of Man (resplendent flashing light) in the heavens.
2. The *redemption* occurs in a sequence of sub-events while the Lord descends (like lightning) from Heaven into Earth's atmosphere:
   a. With a loud command,
   b. With the voice of the archangel,
   c. And with the trumpet call of God:
      i. At the sounding of the last trumpet, the angels are sent to gather his elect from the four winds:
         1. The dead in Christ are first resurrected, transformed, then gathered up to Earth's atmosphere to meet the Lord;
         2. Those in Christ who are still alive when the Lord returns are suddenly transformed then gathered up to Earth's atmosphere to meet the Lord and the others.
      ii. The angels, accompanied by Jesus, transport them all to Heaven to be with the Lord forever.

These outlined sub-events associated with the *day of redemption* were organized and compiled to give a simple, conceptual view of what will occur based on Jesus' teachings from his Olivet Discourse, found in the gospels of Matthew 24:27-31, Mark 13:24-27, and Luke 21:25-28, and from Luke

17:24, as well as the teachings of the Apostle Paul found in 1
Thessalonians 4:13-18.

## Chapter Four

# Rapture vs. Harvest

The term *Harvest* is used in the Parable of the Weeds (Matthew 13:24-43). Jesus explains the meaning of this parable to his disciples—that the *harvest* is the *end of the age*, and that the *harvesters* are *angels*. Jesus tells his disciples that the *weeds* are the *sons of the evil one*, and that the *good seed* represents the *sons of the kingdom*. Jesus clarifies that at the *end of the age*, he [40]"...will send out his angels to weed out of his kingdom everything that causes sin and all who do evil" (the children of the evil one). The angels will gather and cast the evil ones into the fiery furnace, and then gather the righteous who are left, and they will shine like the sun in the kingdom of their Father.

Likewise, from the Parable of the Net (Matthew 13:47-50), Jesus teaches that, at the *end of the age*, the angels will come and separate the wicked (bad fish) from the righteous (good fish) and throw the wicked into the fiery furnace, where there will be weeping and gnashing of teeth.

Matthew 25:31-46 states that "When the Son of Man comes in his glory, and all the angels with him, he will sit on his glorious throne in heavenly glory. All the nations will be gathered before him, and he will separate the people one from another as a shepherd separates the sheep from the

---

[40] Matthew 13:41

73

goats.  He will put the sheep on his right, and the goats will be gathered on his left.  And to the righteous he will say, 'Come you who are blessed by my Father; take your inheritance, the kingdom prepared for you since the creation of the world.'...but he will say to those on his left, 'Depart from me, you who are cursed, into the eternal fire prepared for the devil and his angels.'"  Those on his left will be those who have rejected the righteousness that God had to offer them through faith his beloved son, Jesus, who suffered and died on their behalf, paying a great price to redeem them from the wicked one.  But being so puffed up with pride, they refused God's free gift, and instead chose their own way.

An important distinction to remember, and a major difference between the *rapture* and the *harvest*, is that when Jesus comes back for the first time, three things happen:  (1) the sign of the Son of Man appears bright and resplendent in the heavens, (2) he sends forth his angels with a loud trumpet call, and (3) the angels gather his elect.  Note that *only* his elect are gathered "from the four winds, from one end of the heavens to the other," or, as stated in the Gospel of Mark, [41]"from the ends of the earth to the ends of the heavens." Also, Jesus' first visit is very quick, for it happens in a flash, in the twinkling of an eye.  This is when he comes like a thief to steal away his own, and he only descends into Earth's atmosphere—he doesn't set foot on the ground the first time he comes back.

---

[41] Mark 13:27

The *first gathering* by the angels is associated *only* with the gathering of the *elect*—those who are aligned with God, and who have maintained a faith relationship with him; but when Jesus comes back the [42]second time, he sends forth his angels to gather and to separate the tares from the wheat, the bad fish from the good fish. This *second gathering* is when the living wicked will be separated from all those still living who will have repented, those who will have humbled themselves and will have acknowledged and received the mercy and grace God offered them, and by doing so many will be declared righteous. They will be the children of the kingdom age, those who will repopulate the earth during the millennial reign of Christ with his saints.

So, the *rapture* and the *Harvest* are two distinct and separate events, and they are events that occur at different times as well. Also we see that there are two gatherings—the *first gathering* occurs at the *rapture*, the *second gathering* happens at the *harvest*. It is important to be clear on these issues, because there has been much confusion. Many people think that the *rapture* and the *harvest* are the same event, but they are not.

Something else that should be noted again is that Jesus says the *harvest* is the *end of the age*. For the age of man's reign on Earth ends at the *harvest*, and the age of God's reign on Earth begins after the *harvest*. So, let's summarize all of this again to make sure it is clearly understood:

---

[42] Matthew 25:31-46

*Rapture vs. Harvest*

**The *rapture* is associated with the *last day*,** and the *rapture* deals with both the DEAD AND LIVING RIGHTEOUS— the *elect*. It includes the resurrection and transformation of those who have already died (fallen asleep) in Christ, and it also includes the transformation of those in Christ who are still living when he returns at his *first coming*—at the *rapture*—on the *last day*—at the sounding of the *last trumpet*, just as it says in 1 Thessalonians 4:16-18.

The most important thing to remember here is that the dead *and* the living *righteous* are those who are IN CHRIST! It means they aligned with God, and that they maintained a FAITH RELATIONSHIP with him. Jesus told the five foolish virgins, "...[43]I tell you the truth, I don't know you." And to the lukewarm church at Laodicea he says, [44]"Here I am! I stand at the door and knock. If anyone hears my voice and opens the door, I will come in and eat with him, and he with me."

What door do you think Jesus is talking about when he says, "I stand at the door and knock?" Doesn't it sound like he desires the type of relationship where he comes and meets you where you're at? He is the one who has come to your door. He is the one that is doing the knocking. He waits patiently for you there—waiting for you to invite him in so he can dine with you.

That's fellowship! That's a relationship! And to think this is in a letter that Jesus wrote to the church that thought it was rich, but didn't realize that it was actually "wretched,

---

[43] Matthew 25:12
[44] Revelation 3:20

pitiful, poor, blind and naked" in Jesus' eyes. Perhaps that church overlooked the one thing that was really most important to God.

Do you have a personal relationship with him right now? Notice that the relationship Jesus describes is not a one-way type of relationship. He says, "I will eat *with* him, and he *with* me." It's two-way. A *relationship* with Jesus is the key to being ready and prepared for the *rapture.* Know this also, that when you open your heart's door to Jesus, he will come in and be *with* you—and you can bet you won't ever find him on his cell phone talking to someone else while he's dining with you.

**The *harvest* is associated with the *end of the age*,** and it ONLY involves those who are alive at the time of Jesus' return, when he sets foot on Earth again. It is when both the LIVING righteous and the LIVING wicked will be separated and placed on Jesus' right hand or left hand, respectively.

Then, the living wicked will be cast into the fiery furnace, and the living righteous, who are God's faithful servants, will be rewarded with entry into the kingdom. This *second gathering* occurs after the *time of wrath* has ended— after the seven bowls, filled with the wrath of God, have all been poured out.

So, the *rapture* and *harvest* are not only two *distinct* events—but the *rapture* will PRECEDE the *time of wrath*, and the *harvest* will FOLLOW the *time of wrath*, that *great and terrible day of the Lord*, when God's bowl judgments are poured out over the earth. The *Kingdom Age* then follows the *Harvest*.

### *Rapture* ▸ *Time of Wrath* ▸ *Harvest* ▸ *Kingdom Age*

The *first coming* of the Son of Man is when he comes like a thief in the night, and where the "one shall be taken, and the other left." The Olivet Discourse climaxes with the rapture and redemption event. It is with a loud command, with the voice of the archangel, and with the trumpet call of God that the Son of Man descends from Heaven into Earth's atmosphere, at which time his angels gather his *elect* from the four winds, and they are *caught up* suddenly to meet the Lord in the air, and together they are instantly transported from the Earth-end of the heavens to the Heaven-end of the heavens.

### The Elect

Who are the elect referred to in the Mark 14:27 passage? Some people believe that the *elect* are only Jews, but this does not appear to be the case according to God's word; for the Greek word is [45]*eklektos.* It is used in the New Testament to describe those who have two things in common: they are *aligned* with God, and they have a relationship with him. *Eklektos* is used in reference to Jewish believers, Gentile believers, the good angels, and even our Lord Jesus; so if you

---

[45] See short commentary by Richard H Perry: *Who are the elect?* http://www.lastdaysmystery.info/who_are_the_elect.htm

think the *elect* are only Jews, I strongly recommend you research this one for yourself. Since the good angels are the ones assisting Jesus in the gathering of his elect, and since Jesus is the one coming for his elect, this leaves only Jewish and Gentile believers to be the *elect* Jesus was referring to.

The *second coming* of the **Son of Man** is when he comes [46]riding on a white horse as "King of Kings and Lord of Lords" with the armies of heaven following him, all riding on white horses and dressed in fine linen, white and clean, descending to Earth with [47]great glory. He will immediately [48]destroy the antichrist and the false prophet by casting them alive into the lake of fire, and he will destroy the [49]armies that have gathered at Armageddon to wage war against him by the words that come from his mouth, and he will then sit on his glorious throne.

And at that time, after the *time of wrath*, the nations will be gathered before him. He will send forth his angels to gather the wicked from among the righteous who dwell on the earth, like a shepherd separating the sheep from the goats.

The sheep are given the kingdom, and Jesus reigns as King of Kings and Lord of Lords for a thousand years. The good sheep are those who have survived the *time of wrath* and who afterward enter the millennial kingdom in their natural, human bodies. They are the ones who will be

---

[46] Revelation 19:11-21; 20:1-6
[47] Matthew 25:31-33
[48] Revelation 19:20-20
[49] Revelation 19:19,21

governed by the King of Kings and Lord of Lords, and who will repopulate the earth during the millennium.

The [50]saints who were fully redeemed on the *last day* will be reigning on the earth with Jesus for the thousand years in the *millennial kingdom* as priests of God and of Christ. They will be given thrones and the authority to judge [51]even angels.

### What Do You Believe?

So, what do *you* believe about the return of the Lord? Does Jesus return only once, or does he actually come back twice? Does the Bible clearly make this distinction between the *rapture* and the *harvest*? Does the Son of Man come back for everyone who calls himself a Christian, or does he only come for those who have been waiting and watching for his return, those he knows, and who know him, who are aligned with him, and who are ready to leave this life behind? Remember, in the [52]Ten Virgins Parable, all ten virgins fell asleep—yet five still went in to be with the bridegroom, even though they *all* fell asleep. The only difference was that five were *prepared* to meet him and the bridegroom knew who they were, so only those five went *in* to the wedding banquet; the other five went *out* to buy their own oil. What did Jesus say to the five foolish virgins, after the door had already been

---

[50] Revelation 20:4,6
[51] 1 Corinthians 6:3
[52] Matthew 25:1-13

shut, who afterward came to him?—[53]"Truly I tell you, I don't know you."

It's wonderful that so many believers believe Jesus will be coming back! But understand that *what* a person believes about the Lord's coming is beneficial only if what they believe about it actually turns out to be correct, and if they are ready—and this is especially true regarding the *rapture*, when he comes as a [54]thief in the [55]night.

That's why we must be very careful to perceive the truth from the scriptures, and to make sure that we are not simply trusting and believing in what we have been told by others, no matter how honest, legitimate or credentialed someone may appear to be. Something *this* important should come straight from the Lord. The Bible says to [56]"continue to work out your salvation with fear and trembling, for it is God who works in you to will and to act in order to fulfill his good purpose." Jesus wants you to enter-in when he comes—will your ears perceive what God has to say, and will your heart be willing to obey the voice of the Spirit concerning these things of God?

It is important that we read and meditate on God's word for ourselves, and that we not expect to borrow the oil of others like the five foolish virgins did. We must do our own homework, making sure that we are not wandering into

---

[53] Matthew 25:12
[54] Revelation 15:16
[55] Luke 17:34
[56] Philippians 2:12-13

speculative territory, or making false assumptions that can lead us and others astray. It's very easy to do this—especially if you've been brought up to believe what you are taught, without first asking God what he thinks.

It is essential to listen to what Jesus has to say first about the events, or signs, that signify his coming, and then to listen to what he has to say about his *actual* coming—as the thief in the night, or as the King of Kings and Lord of Lords, riding on a white horse with the armies of heaven following after him.

And then finally, we should compare what we learn from specific scriptures with what other scriptures of the same context have to say in order to make certain we are looking at the complete picture as the Lord presents it, as the prophets declared it, and as apostles also enlightened us in their accounts and letters as well.

Jesus spent a lot of time teaching his disciples about what his return would be like, and how to prepare for it. And that is an excellent place to start in order to understand God's point of view in all of this—beginning with what Jesus taught his disciples! That is why this book started with the Merged Gospel Narrative of Jesus' Olivet Discourse, along with his other teachings.

Dive into the scriptures so you will find the answers to your many questions concerning the coming of the Lord, and hear first-hand from God's word what Jesus has to say about it all. For Jesus says, [57]"Ask and it will be given to you; seek and you will find; knock and the door will be opened to you, for everyone who asks receives; he who seeks finds; and to him who knocks, the door will be opened."

In the next chapters of this book, we will be discussing other rapture-related topics found elsewhere in the Bible to see how they compare with what Jesus taught his disciples. Appendix A contains the Merged Gospel Narrative without all the comments. Appendix B has many of the rapture-related scriptures gathered together for your convenience. Again, it is most important that you study for yourself, believing God in faith that he will reveal to you the answers to your questions, and other things he wants you to know.

---

[57] Matthew 7:7-8

## Chapter Five

# Daniel Sequence
### *The Ruler, the Anointed One, and The Ruler Who Will Come*

## *Daniel Chapter 9*

The angel Gabriel spoke to Daniel declaring, "Seventy 'sevens' are decreed for your people and your holy city to finish transgression, to put an end to sin, to atone for wickedness, to bring in everlasting righteousness, to seal up vision and prophecy and to anoint the Most Holy Place." Of the Seventy "sevens" prophesied by Daniel, sixty-nine of those sevens have already been fulfilled. Daniel 9:24 makes it very clear that "the abomination that causes desolation" event occurs in the middle of that seventieth "seven", or seventieth "week" of Daniel.

So, "Seventy sevens" have been decreed for the Jewish people and their holy city, Jerusalem, to accomplish the following God-objectives:

1. Finish transgression
2. Put an end to sin
3. Atone for wickedness
4. Bring in everlasting righteousness
5. Seal up vision and prophecy
6. Anoint the Most Holy Place.

*Daniel Sequence*

The "sevens" are weeks of years. These are Jewish years of 360 days each. Chapter 9 of the Book of Daniel places the "abomination that causes desolation" event as occurring in the middle of the seventieth week, or 1260 days (3.5 years x 360 days per year = 1260 days) after the beginning of the seventieth week. The seventieth week of *Daniel* begins when the "ruler who will come" confirms a [58]"covenant with many for one seven," or seven Jewish years.

Note that *Daniel Chapter 9* mentions two rulers: The first is the [59]"Anointed One, the ruler." The second is the [60]"ruler who will come." The "Anointed One, the ruler" is cut-off [killed] after sixty-nine sevens are completed. The second "ruler who will come" is the one that "confirms a covenant with many" and who perpetrates the "abomination that causes desolation" in the middle of the seventieth week of Daniel.

The Apostle Paul, in 2 Thessalonians, has some interesting information to add regarding this "ruler who will come." Paul writes on behalf of the apostles to the Thessalonians, in order to clear up an issue that was happening where some of the men in the church were not working because they thought Jesus could return at any moment. So Paul wrote to the Thessalonians "concerning the coming of our Lord Jesus Christ and our being gathered to him."

---

[58] Daniel 9:27
[59] Daniel 9:25
[60] Daniel 9:26b

Paul tells them:

[61]"...not to become easily unsettled or alarmed by some prophecy, report or letter supposed to have come from us, saying that the *day of the Lord* has already come. Don't let anyone deceive you in any way, for that day [*day of the Lord*] will not come until the rebellion occurs and the man of lawlessness is revealed, the man doomed to destruction. He will oppose and will exalt himself over everything that is called God or is worshiped, so that he sets himself up in God's temple, proclaiming himself to be God."

Paul continues:

[62]"Don't you remember that when I was with you I used to tell you these things? And now you know what is holding him back, so that he may be revealed at the proper time. For the secret power of lawlessness is already at work; but the one who now holds it back will continue to do so till he is taken out of the way. And then the lawless one will be revealed whom the Lord Jesus will overthrow with the breath of his mouth and destroy by the splendor of his coming. The coming of the lawless one will be in accordance with the work of Satan displayed in all kinds of counterfeit miracles, signs and wonders, and in every sort of evil that deceives those who are perishing. They perish

---

[61] 2 Thessalonians 2:1-4
[62] 2 Thessalonians 2:5-12

because they refused to love the truth and so be saved. For this reason God sends them a powerful delusion so that they will believe the lie and so that all will be condemned who have not believed the truth but have delighted in wickedness."

First of all, Paul made it very clear to the Thessalonian believers that the *day of the Lord* had not happened yet, and that it would not occur until AFTER the rebellion and AFTER the *man of lawlessness* is revealed. Remember, the topic of Paul's letter at this point is the *rapture*, or, as Paul called it, "the coming of our Lord Jesus Christ and our being gathered to meet him." Since the basis of Paul's argument in 2 Thessalonians, Chapter 2, makes the assumption that the *day of the Lord* will precede "the coming of our Lord Jesus Christ and our being gathered to meet him," it would certainly be reasonable, then, to assume the Thessalonian believers already knew that the *day of the Lord* was supposed to occur *prior* to the "*being gathered to meet him.*"

It was because some people in the church were teaching that the *day of the Lord* had already occurred, that some of the men in the church were deceived and thought they should stop working, and instead, be [63]lifting up their heads like Jesus said to do, for they thought their redemption was about to take place at any moment. That redemption

---

[63] Matthew 21:28

being the redemption of their bodies, for their souls and spirits were already redeemed by Christ's blood.

Realize that those who stopped working *knew* that the *day of the Lord* was to occur *before* the *rapture*, yet they did not actually *see* it occur themselves—instead, they believed what was being taught by false teachers within the church. So Paul helped these men to realize that the *day of the Lord* had indeed *not* happened yet, because the specific events that were to precede the *day of the Lord* had also *not yet* occurred—i.e. the rebellion, and the revealing of the man of lawlessness. Paul continued to detail these preceding events by describing to them an event that sounds very much like the *abomination that causes desolation*, an event perpetrated by the "man doomed to destruction, whom the Lord Jesus will overthrow with the breath of his mouth and destroy by the splendor of his coming."

Let's now take a closer look at the Daniel 9:25-27 passage. It appears that the events of this passage are sequential—that is, they are progressive through time:

"Know and understand this: From the time the word goes out to restore and rebuild Jerusalem until the Anointed One, the ruler, comes, there will be seven 'sevens,' and sixty-two 'sevens.' It will be rebuilt with streets and a trench, but in times of trouble. After the sixty-two 'sevens,' the Anointed One will be put to death and will have nothing. The people of the ruler who will come will destroy the city and the sanctuary. The end will come like a flood: War will continue until the end, and desolations have been decreed. He will confirm a covenant with many for one 'seven.' In the middle of the 'seven' he will put an end to sacrifice and offering. And at the temple he will set up an *abomination that causes desolation*, until the end that is decreed is poured out on him."

So, in *Daniel Chapter 9*, we see the following sequence of events unfold:

1. The word goes out to restore and rebuild Jerusalem.
2. It is rebuilt with streets and a trench, but in times of trouble.
3. Seven sevens and sixty-two sevens of time pass (49 + 434 = 483 years).
4. The Anointed One is put to death and has nothing.
5. The people of the ruler who will come destroy the city [Jerusalem] and the sanctuary [the temple].
6. **War continues, and desolations are decreed.**
7. He [the ruler who will come] confirms [or strengthens] a covenant with many for one 'seven.'
8. In the middle of the 'seven' [3 ½ years, or 1260 days] he puts an end to sacrifice and offering. He [the ruler who will come] sets up an *abomination that causes desolation* at the temple [a new, future third temple].

9. The end comes like a flood—the end that is decreed is poured out on him [the ruler who will come].

Of the nine events that make up the *Daniel Chapter 9* sequence, the first five events have already taken place. The sixth event (boldface type) began when the temple was destroyed in 70 A.D., and since that time, war and desolations have continued to this day; however, the last three events, events 7 through 9, are all future events still to unfold—Jesus clarifies this by making reference to them in his Olivet Discourse, where he also states the *abomination that causes desolation* by name, and cites the name of the prophet who prophesied the event he was referring to—Daniel.

The sequences of both Daniel and Jesus align at the *abomination that causes desolation* event, the eighth event of Daniel's Chapter 9 Sequence. In fact, you can actually insert all the Jesus sequences of parts 5 and 6 of Chapter 2, which are the "Abomination that Causes Desolation" and the "Day of the Lord" events, in between event numbers 8 and 9 of the *Daniel Chapter 9* sequence to combine them as one larger sequence.

Although there are other sequences in the Book of Daniel, the Daniel Chapter 9 sequence is sufficient for the topic of the *rapture*. The books of Daniel, and especially Revelation, are filled with many end-times event sequences, but for the sake of keeping this simple, this is the only reference we will use from the Book of Daniel.

# Chapter Six

# When the Stars Fall

A day is coming when [64]"the sun will be darkened and the moon will not give its light. At that time the stars will fall from the sky, and heavenly bodies will be shaken. There will be [65]signs in the sun, moon and stars. On the earth, nations will be in anguish and perplexity at the roaring and tossing of the sea. Men will faint from terror, apprehensive of what is coming on the world, for the heavenly bodies will be shaken."

[66]"When these things begin to take place, stand up and lift up your heads, because your redemption is drawing near. For then will appear the sign of the Son of Man in heaven." [67]"Men will see the Son of Man coming in clouds with great power and glory! And then all the peoples of the earth will mourn when they see the Son of Man coming on the clouds of heaven, with power and great glory."

[68]"He will send his angels with a loud trumpet call, and they will gather his elect from the four winds, from one end of the heavens to the other. [69]On that day no one who is on the roof of his house, with his goods inside, should go down to get

---

[64] Matthew 24:29
[65] Luke 21:25-26
[66] Luke 21:28
[67] Mark 13:26
[68] Matthew 24:31
[69] Luke 17:30-35

them. Likewise, no one in the field should go back for anything. Remember Lot's wife! Whoever tries to keep his life will lose it, and whoever loses his life will preserve it. I tell you, on that night two people will be in one bed; one will be taken and the other left. Two women will be grinding grain together; one will be taken and the other left."

[70]"Be careful, or your hearts will be weighed down with dissipation, drunkenness and the anxieties of this life, and that day will close on you unexpectedly like a trap. For it will come upon all those who live on the face of the whole earth. Be always on the watch, and pray that you may be able to escape all that is about to happen, and that you may be able to stand before the Son of Man."

Those are Jesus' words. Do you hear what he is saying? "The sun will be darkened"—"the moon will not give its light"—"the stars will fall from the sky"—"nations will be in anguish and perplexity at the roaring and tossing of the sea"— "men will faint from terror, apprehensive of what is coming on the world, for the heavenly bodies will be shaken—for then will appear the sign of the Son of Man in heaven!"

These are all Jesus' words, and they are the key events that Jesus says will take place immediately before the "one will be taken, and the other left" event takes place just hours later—in the [71]evening of that same day. For immediately after [72]these events occur, Jesus said that he would send his

---

[70] Luke 21:34-36
[71] Luke 17:34
[72] Matthew 24:29-31; Mark 13:24-27; Luke 21:25-28

angels "with a loud trumpet call," and that they would "gather his elect from the four winds, from one end of the heavens to the other."

Wow!—this is a lot to take in and to process in one's mind for sure. And these scriptures are only dealing with the gathering of the church to meet the Lord in the air—the *rapture-redemption*. When you consider how significant and impacting these sign events are that immediately precede our Lord's return, they can be quite frightening indeed, to say the least, to visualize them in your mind.

What will the people of this world think when these sign events begin to take place? If they don't know what is happening, most will probably think it is the end of the world, or worse—judgment day! Remember, the *day of the Lord* will be a dreadful day for those who do not know the Lord. Men will faint "from terror, apprehensive of what is coming on the world..." But we should not be afraid as those who have no hope. This will be a glorious day of redemption for those in Christ, who aligned with God, who love him and have a relationship with him. This is the day they have been waiting and watching for!

The Bible says that [73]"you will know the truth, and the truth shall set you free." I am convinced that when we fear something, we become controlled, or subdued, by whatever it is we fear. There is freedom in finding the truth about those things that frightens us. That is why it is important to share

---

[73] John 8:32

genuine truth with others. Jesus often said, "Truly, truly I say to you..."

It's time to bring things together, now that we have become more familiar with many of the scriptures and terms surrounding this wonderful *rapture-redemption* event. Let's move on, then, and see how the writings of the apostles and the prophets contribute to, and harmonize with, what Jesus had to say about this amazing event:

## Chapter Seven

# What is God Saying?

### *Trumpet Call of God*

When Jesus said in Matthew 24:31, that he would send his angels with a loud trumpet call, he really didn't say *what* loud trumpet call he was referring to. So then, *what* loud trumpet call would Jesus have been referring to here?

Perhaps the Apostle Paul can shed some light on this mystery for us, since he also had several things to say about this same subject. In 1 Thessalonians 4:16-17, Paul writes, "For the Lord himself will come down from heaven, with a [74]loud command, with the voice of the archangel and with the trumpet call of God, and the dead in Christ will rise first. After that, we who are still alive and are left will be caught up together with them in the clouds to meet the Lord in the air. And so we will be with the Lord forever."

Paul, here, clarifies three things for us: First, that those who have died in Christ will be resurrected, and that they will be the first ones to meet the Lord in the air when

---

[74] Greek word, "Keleuma", meaning an order, command, spec. a stimulating cry, either that by which animals are roused and urged on by man, as horses by charioteers, hounds by hunters, etc., or that by which a signal is given to men, e.g. to rowers by the master of a ship, to soldiers by a commander (with a loud summons, a trumpet call). From The KJV New Testament Greek Lexicon; Strong's Number: 2752.

Jesus comes. After those who are dead-in-Christ have first been *caught up*, then those who are in Christ, that are still alive at the coming of the Lord, will also suddenly be *caught up* together with them to meet the Lord in the air. In other words, Paul has connected the gathering of those who have died in Christ with the gathering of those who are still living and are in Christ at the time of his coming.

Secondly, Paul, in 1 Corinthians 15:51-52, further clarifies these events by writing, "Listen, I tell you a mystery: We will not all sleep, but we will all be changed—in a flash, in the twinkling of an eye, at the last trumpet. For the trumpet will sound, the dead will be raised imperishable, and we will be changed." Notice that Paul moreover clarifies here that the trumpet call of God is also the *last trumpet*. So then, these events will not only take place at the sound of a trumpet, but it will take place at the sound of the *last trumpet*—so what "last" trumpet could Paul have been referring to here in this passage? We'll get to this soon.

Thirdly, Paul gives us the order of events that will occur immediately preceding the *rapture*: (1) A loud command [shout], (2) the voice of the archangel, and (3) the trumpet call of God. So at the sounding of *the last trumpet*...the dead in Christ will rise first; then those in Christ who are alive and remain will also suddenly be caught up together with them to meet the Lord in the air—the *rapture!*

Since these are all future events that have not occurred yet, wouldn't it make sense to go to the Book of Revelation and consider what John prophesied concerning this loud command [shout], the voice of the archangel, and *the last trumpet*?

# *The Mighty Angel*

In Revelation, Chapter Ten, a mighty angel comes down from heaven and gives "a loud shout like the roar of a lion." This doesn't necessarily mean that the angel's shout sounds like a lion's roar, but rather that the volume of his shout is like the volume of a lion's roar. He shouts so loud that the seven thunders also speak, saying something John is not permitted to write down for us. After this mighty angel shouts, he then declares over the earth, "There will be no more delay!" Immediately following that declaration at the end of Revelation 10:6 the next sentence reads, [75]"When the seventh angel blows his trumpet God's mysterious plan will be fulfilled. It will happen just as he announced it to his servants the prophets."

So this mighty angel first shouts and then declares, "There will be no more delay!" No more delay of what? Could this be the answer to the question asked in Revelation 6:9-11 by all the souls of those slain because of the word of God and the testimony they had maintained, who called out from beneath the altar in heaven saying, "How long, Sovereign Lord, holy and true, until you judge the inhabitants of the earth and avenge our blood?" John then tells us, "They were given white robes and told to wait a little longer, until the

---

[75] Revelation 10:7 (NLT); Note also that "God's mysterious plan" is translated "the mystery of God" in the NIV.

number of their fellow servants and brothers who were to be killed as they had been was completed."

Could the declaration of this mighty angel mean that the long wait of these souls beneath the altar may finally be over?—considering especially that it is after this mighty angel makes God's declaration, "There will be no more delay!" that the seventh angel then blasts his trumpet—*the last trumpet* of Revelation! So will God now judge the inhabitants of the earth and avenge the blood of those martyred souls who cried out to God from beneath the altar in heaven? Is it now the time for God's wrath to begin to be poured out upon the earth?

In 2 Thessalonians 1:5-7, Paul lets the suffering believers know that: "God's judgment is right, and as a result you will be counted worthy of the kingdom of God, for which you are suffering. God is just: He will pay back trouble to those who trouble you and give relief to you who are troubled, and to us as well. This will happen when the Lord Jesus is revealed from heaven in blazing fire with his powerful angels. He will punish those who do not know God and do not obey the gospel of our Lord Jesus. They will be punished with everlasting destruction and shut out from the presence of the Lord and from the glory of his might on the day he comes to be glorified in his holy people and to be marveled at among all those who have believed."

But what about this mighty angel who declares, "There will be no more delay!"—Do you think that this mighty angel could very well be an archangel?—and if so, could he be the archangel that the Apostle Paul was referring to? After all, he is called a *mighty* angel, and he sounds enormous!

John describes him like this in Revelation 10:1-2, 5: "Then I saw another mighty angel coming down from heaven. He was robed in a cloud, with a rainbow above his head; his face was like the sun, and his legs were like fiery pillars. He was holding a little scroll, which lay open in his hand. He planted his right foot on the sea and his left foot on the land, and he gave a loud shout like the roar of a lion." "Then the angel I had seen standing on the sea and on the land raised his right hand to heaven. And he swore by him who lives for ever and ever, who created the heavens and all that is in them, the earth and all that is in it, and the sea and all that is in it, and said, 'There will be no more delay!'"

If this mighty angel is the archangel that the Apostle Paul was referring to, then could the *shout* of this mighty angel, that was so strong that it caused the seven thunders to speak, also be the *loud command* Paul was referring to? Could the mighty voice that declared, "There will be no more delay!" be the voice of the archangel Paul was referring to? And could the seventh and last trumpet of Revelation be the *trumpet call of God* and the *last trumpet* that both Jesus and Paul were referring to?

Keeping these things in mind, read 1 Thessalonians 4:16-17: "[16] For the Lord himself will come down from heaven, with a loud command [shout], with the voice of the archangel and with the trumpet call of God, and the dead in Christ will rise first. [17] After that, we who are still alive and are left will be caught up together with them in the clouds to meet the Lord in the air. And so we will be with the Lord forever."

Also read 1 Corinthians 15:51-52 again: "Listen, I tell you a mystery: We will not all sleep, but we will all be changed—in a flash, in the twinkling of an eye, at *the last trumpet*. For the trumpet will sound, the dead will be raised imperishable, and we will be changed."

It is interesting that in Revelation 11:15, immediately after the seventh trumpet of Revelation finishes sounding, the first thing that happens is that loud voices are heard in heaven declaring, [76]"The kingdom of the world has become the kingdom of our Lord and of his Christ, and he will reign for ever and ever."—Yes, it's the Hallelujah Chorus! Notice here that it says the "kingdom" of the world, and not the "kingdoms" of the world. When Jesus was tempted by the devil in the [77]wilderness, the devil offered Jesus the "kingdoms" of the world and all their splendor, but now—by the seventh trumpet of Revelation—the world seems to have become only one kingdom—a one world government—doesn't that sound familiar?

Immediately after the loud voices in heaven are heard saying, [78]"The kingdom of the world has become the kingdom of our Lord and of his Christ, and he will reign for ever and ever," Revelation 11:16-17 says that "the twenty-four elders, who were seated on their thrones before God, fell on their

---

[76] Revelation 11:15
[77] Luke 4:5
[78] Revelation 11:15

faces and worshiped God, saying: 'We give thanks to you, Lord God Almighty, the One who is and who was, because you have taken your great power and have begun to reign.'"

So, after the sounding of the seventh trumpet of Revelation, it has become the day when the Lord takes his authority and begins to reign from heaven first! The twenty-four elders also say in verse 18 that "The nations were angry; and your wrath has come. The time has come for judging the dead, and for rewarding your servants the prophets and your saints and those who reverence your name, both small and great—and for destroying those who destroy the earth." Yes, the seventh trumpet is associated with several events that occur both in heaven *and* on the earth.

After the blast of the seventh trumpet of Revelation, the kingdom of the world will have become the kingdom of our Lord and of his Christ. He will then reign for ever and ever, and it is the *first* day when Jesus has "taken his great power and has begun to reign." Wouldn't it be logical to assume that it is also the *last day* of mankind's reign over the earth?

And if the seventh trumpet of Revelation is indeed *the last trumpet* and the *trumpet call of God* that both Jesus and the Apostle Paul were referring to, during which blast the *rapture* takes place, wouldn't that day of the resurrection also be *the last day* that Jesus was referring to in the Book of St. John, where he referred to it four times? [79]"And this is the will

---

[79] John 6:39

of him who sent me, that I shall lose none of all those he has given me, but raise them up at the *last day*. [80]For my Father's will is that everyone who looks to the Son and believes in him shall have eternal life, and I will raise them up at the *last day*." [81]"No one can come to me unless the Father who sent me draws them, and I will raise them up at the *last day*. [82]Whoever eats my flesh and drinks my blood has eternal life, and I will raise them up at the *last day*.

Since the resurrection occurs at the *last day* according to Jesus, and since the resurrection is part of the gathering of the saints [the *rapture*] according to Paul, and since the gathering of the saints occurs at the sounding of the *last trumpet* according to Paul, and since the mighty angel of Revelation declares, "There will be no more delay." "[83]But in the days of the voice of the seventh angel, when he shall *begin* to sound the trumpet, the mystery of God shall be finished, as he hath declared by his servants the prophets," and, [84]since the only *mystery of God* in the entire Bible associated with a *last trumpet* is found in 1 Corinthians 15:51-52, then, when the seventh angel *begins* to sound his trumpet, and before it is completed, God's elect will be "gathered from the four winds, from the ends of the earth to the ends of the heavens" to be forever with the Lord.

---

[80] John 6:40
[81] John 6:44
[82] John 6:54
[83] Revelation 10:7 (Douay-Rheims 1899 American Edition)
[84] See Appendix D, **Revelation 10:7 *Interpretation*** for more detailed comments regarding the translation of this verse of scripture.

And *after* the seventh angel has sounded his trumpet, it will be the time when "The kingdom of the world has become the kingdom of our Lord and of his Christ, and he will reign for ever and ever," and the twenty-four elders who were seated on their thrones before God, fell on their faces and worshiped God, giving thanks and said, "you have taken your great power and have begun to reign," and "The nations were angry; and your wrath has come. The time has come for judging the dead, and for rewarding your servants the prophets and your saints and those who reverence your name, both small and great—and for destroying those who destroy the earth." Afterward, "God's temple in heaven was opened, and within his temple was seen the ark of his covenant. And there came flashes of lightning, rumblings, peals of thunder, an earthquake and a great hailstorm."

Doesn't what takes place in heaven after the sounding of the seventh trumpet of Revelation seem very much like Jesus' coronation? For this is the time when Jesus takes his power and begins to reign—in heaven first! And isn't it interesting to think that since the elect are gathered or snatched away by the angels from the four winds to meet Jesus in the air, and afterward they are then instantly transported "from the ends of the earth to the ends of the heavens," that they, along with Jesus, would arrive in heaven just in time to enjoy the Hallelujah Chorus and our Lord's coronation ceremony!—for the *rapture* happens in an instant.

But immediately following that wonderful event in heaven, Revelation 11:19 declares, "Then God's temple in heaven was opened, and within his temple was seen the ark of his covenant." This is just like at the Battle of Jericho, where the seven priests each carrying a trumpet preceded the Ark of the Covenant that manifested the presence of God!

Unfortunately for those people still dwelling on the earth after the *rapture* takes place, Revelation 15:5 then states: "After this I looked and in heaven the temple, that is, the tabernacle of the Testimony, was opened. Out of the temple came the seven angels with the seven plagues...Then one of the four living creatures gave to the seven angels seven golden bowls filled with the wrath of God, who lives for ever and ever. And the temple was filled with smoke from the glory of God and from his power, and no one could enter the temple until the seven plagues of the seven angels were completed."

Notice what occurs *after* the seventh trumpet sounds: Jesus takes his authority and begins to reign; the kingdom of this earth becomes the kingdom of our Lord and of his Christ. This, then, is followed by the *time of wrath* where the seven bowls filled with the wrath of God are poured out by each of the seven angels in succession as God "judges those who destroy the earth."

Doesn't it make sense that at the sounding of the seventh trumpet that the saints should be delivered from the impending wrath of God just like Rahab, the harlot, was delivered from the destruction of the wall of Jericho and God's impending judgment on the people of Jericho? For the scripture declares in 1 Thessalonians 5:9, "For God did not appoint us to suffer wrath but to receive salvation through our Lord Jesus Christ." And Jesus tells us in Luke 21:36, to "Be always on the watch, and pray that you may be able to escape all that is about to happen, and that you may be able to stand before the Son of Man." It is amazing how God does things— how he speaks through so many different prophets; yet everything fits together like a well-fitted puzzle!

# *Ramifications*

The important thing to learn is that we need to be prepared to *leave* this life behind so we don't find ourselves *left* behind. We need to be waiting and watching for that last day, when the sun turns to darkness and when the moon does not give its light—when the stars fall, and when his sign appears in the heavens. We need to know *what* to do when we recognize that this long-awaited day has finally arrived!

We must be obedient to our Lord when he tells us, "When these things begin to take place, stand up and lift up your heads, because your redemption is drawing near." We need to obey him when he says, "On that day no one who is on the roof of his house, with his goods inside, should go down to get them. Likewise, no one in the field should go back for anything. Remember Lot's wife!" We must realize what Jesus means when he says, "Whoever tries to keep his life will lose it, and whoever loses his life will preserve it." For "...on that night two people will be in one bed; one will be taken and the other left. Two women will be grinding grain together; one will be taken and the other left."

We need to practice self-discipline, for Jesus says, "Be careful, or your hearts will be weighed down with dissipation, drunkenness and the anxieties of this life, and *that* day will close on you unexpectedly like a trap." We need to take heed ourselves, and we should warn others, "...For it will come upon all those who live on the face of the whole earth."

And when Jesus tells us, "Be always on the watch, and *pray* that you may be able to escape all that is about to happen, and that you may be able to stand before the Son of Man," we need to take him at his word, and do just that.

We must especially heed his warning to "Remember Lot's wife!" For it was intended that Lot and his whole family be spared from God's judgment on those wicked cities, Sodom and Gomorrah. Lot and his family were given specific instructions not to look back. But his wife disobeyed—she looked back—and she perished.

Lot and his family were not the only ones to be given special instructions, for Noah and his family were instructed to go inside the ark on the day when God's judgment fell—in fact, they were told a week in advance that God's judgment was coming! And the Israelites in Egypt—they were instructed to apply the lamb's blood to their doorposts and to stay inside their dwellings the day God sent the death angel throughout Egypt. If an Israelite family disobeyed God's instructions, they would not have been spared. There is a pattern that can be seen here—that those faithful ones who obeyed God's instructions were spared the fate of the impending judgment on the wicked. So, if *they* didn't obey God's instructions, and if *we* don't—well, just remember Lot's wife!

Remember also that the Israelites were delivered from the Red Sea judgment just prior to God's judgment or wrath being poured out over Pharaoh's army! The Israelites safely crossed over to the other side of the Red Sea as on dry ground, but Pharaoh's army bogged down, and they were swallowed up by the Red Sea, and they *all* perished.

Sometimes Old Testament scriptures unlock New Testament meanings and vice versa. A good example of this is the Battle of Jericho. This event is similar to what takes place in Heaven during the trumpet judgments of Revelation, chapters 8-11. Joshua 6:6 says that "Joshua...called the priests and said to them, 'Take up the ark of the covenant of the Lord and have seven priests carry trumpets in front of it.'" And like the Battle of Jericho, the seven trumpets of Revelation also precede the Ark of the Covenant—yet this time it takes place in the future, and it occurs up in heaven.

On the seventh day, which was *the last day* before judgment fell on Jericho, on "The seventh time around, when the priests sounded the trumpet blast, Joshua commanded the people, 'Shout! For the Lord has given you the city!'" So, on that *last day*, after going around the City of Jericho for the seventh time, there was a *loud command* given by Joshua, and the people of Israel then began *shouting*. And the scripture says, [85]"When the trumpets sounded, the people shouted, and at the sound of the trumpet, when the people gave a loud shout, the wall collapsed." The people of Israel were rewarded that day for their faithfulness, but the City of Jericho experienced God's judgment!

Also on that same day another fascinating parallel occurred. This parallel has to do with the *rapture*. I am speaking of Rahab, the harlot, and her relatives, how they were delivered from God's wrath on Jericho that day when the wall of Jericho fell. Rahab recognized, respected and aligned with the God of the Israelites. She knew about God's judgment on the other cities that had been in the path of the Hebrew people. She made a covenant with the Hebrew spies that came to her City of Jericho. She agreed to hide them if she and her family would be spared. The spies agreed, but gave her specific instructions. All her relatives had to be in her house in the wall, and she had to place a scarlet cord in her window, or else they would perish along with all the others. She and her family did as they were told.

It is interesting that a cord is something that binds, and so is a covenant. Now scarlet, besides being more than just the color of a harlot, also represents blood in the Old Testament. Remember that it was lamb's blood (scarlet) that also saved the Israelites from the death angel of Egypt, but only if the Israelites placed it on their doorposts. It saved Rahab and her family, and it is also the blood of Jesus Christ,

---

[85] Joshua 6:20

the Lamb of God, that brings us deliverance and salvation from the wrath and judgment of God. For we are told in 1 Thessalonians 1:10, "...to wait for his Son from heaven, whom he raised from the dead—Jesus, who rescues us from the coming *wrath*." God says, [86]"Whoever believes in the Son has eternal life, but whoever rejects the Son will not see life, for God's wrath remains on them." God offers deliverance and salvation for us all. In Isaiah 1:18, God says through the prophet, "Come now, let us settle the matter," says the Lord. "Though your sins are like scarlet, they shall be as white as snow; though they are red as crimson, they shall be like wool." It is only through the blood of the Lamb of God, that those who are waiting and watching for the Lord's return will one day be saved from the coming wrath of God. When that day comes, the wrath of God will be unleashed upon the wicked— it would be best not to be down here then.

We must never forget what that day will look like when "the sun will be darkened, and the moon will not give its light." For at that time "the stars will fall from the sky, and heavenly bodies will be shaken. There will be signs in the sun, moon and stars. On the earth, nations will be in anguish and perplexity at the roaring and tossing of the sea. Men will faint from terror, apprehensive of what is coming on the world." We need to remember what it means—*when the stars fall.*

When these things begin to take place, stand up and lift up your heads, because your redemption draws near. Men

---

[86] John 3:36

111

will see the Son of Man coming in clouds with great power and glory! "For then will appear the sign of the Son of Man in heaven. And then all the peoples of the earth will mourn when they see the Son of Man coming on the clouds of heaven, with power and great glory. He will send his angels with a loud trumpet call, and they will gather his elect from the four winds, from one end of the heavens to the other."

"**On that day** no one who is on the roof of his house, with his goods inside, should go down to get them. Likewise, no one in the field should go back for anything. Remember Lot's wife! Whoever tries to keep his life will lose it, and whoever loses his life will preserve it. I tell you, **on that night** two people will be in one bed; one will be taken and the other left. Two women will be grinding grain together; one will be taken and the other left."

"Be careful, or your hearts will be weighed down with dissipation, drunkenness and the anxieties of this life, and that day will close on you unexpectedly like a trap. For it will come upon all those who live on the face of the *whole* earth. Be always on the watch, and pray that you may be able to escape all that is about to happen, and that you may be able to stand before the Son of Man."

We must be waiting and watching for his return! For the scriptures never promise that Christians won't experience tribulation. I have not found a scripture that says Christians won't be here when the trumpet plagues come. See if you can find a scripture that says the trumpet plagues are the *wrath* of

God. It appears that *only* the bowl judgments are associated with the *wrath* of God.

In fact, it is immediately after the sounding of the seventh trumpet of Revelation that the twenty-four elders, who were seated on their thrones before God, fall on their faces and worship God, saying: "We give thanks to you, Lord God Almighty, the One who is and who was, because you have taken your great power and have begun to reign. The nations were angry; and *your wrath has come*. The time has come for judging the dead, and for rewarding your servants the prophets and your saints and those who reverence your name, both small and great—and *for destroying those who destroy the earth*."

After this, the ark of God's covenant appears in the heavenly temple and the seven angels are given the *seven golden bowls filled with the wrath of God*. The heavenly temple is then filled with the smoke from the glory of God and from his power, and no one can enter the temple until the seven plagues of the seven angels are completed. The seven angels are then told to "Go, pour out the *seven bowls of God's wrath* on the earth." Remember this occurs *after* the seventh trumpet has already sounded!

The Apostle Paul also said in 1 Thessalonians 5:1-4: "Now, brothers and sisters, about times and dates we do not need to write to you, for you know very well that the *day of the Lord* will come like a thief in the night. While people are saying, "Peace and safety," destruction will come on them suddenly, as labor pains on a pregnant woman, and they will not escape. But you, brothers and sisters, are not in darkness so that this day should surprise you like a thief." And in verse 9 Paul continues, "For God did not appoint us to suffer *wrath* but to receive salvation through our Lord Jesus Christ."

Now don't be thinking the first time you see unusual darkness, that it is for *sure* the *day of the Lord*; for before the pre-rapture events take place on the *day of the Lord*, there will be other events that will have already occurred that will have impacted the earth already. We will only discuss those events that *most* resemble the *day of the Lord,* so as not to become confused by them. These are events that impede or impact the natural celestial light shining on the earth—that is, the light coming from the sun, the moon and the stars.

The first of those earlier "darkness" events is the fourth trumpet plague, where "a third of the sun was struck, a third of the moon, and a third of the stars, so that a third of them turned dark. A third of the day was without light, and also a third of the night."

A good way to understand the fourth trumpet plague is to consider that a day and night are twenty-four hours long. During this plague, each day and each night will have one third less natural celestial light. Twenty-four hours divided by three (one third less) equals eight hours of absolute natural celestial darkness. That means no sun, no moon and no stars for eight hours of each twenty-four hour day. It won't matter where you live in the world, whether Ecuador or the North Pole, because one third of the daytime plus one third of the nighttime will always be eight hours long.

114

So in Denton, Texas, a 24-hour day in [87]June after the fourth trumpet judgment begins will consist of the following: about six hours of sunlight, followed by ten hours of starlight along with some portion of the moon phase, except when it's the new moon, and then eight hours of absolute celestial darkness. Only six hours of sunlight!

So if a storm covers the celestial sky with clouds during the regular nighttime hours, then the period of absolute celestial darkness could even seem longer than eight hours on those days. The Bible is not clear whether this fourth trumpet plague will continue past the fifth trumpet plague or not.

Then, after the fifth angel sounds his trumpet, the Bible says that the light of the sun, moon and stars will be reduced by the smoke that rises up from the Abyss. The Bible doesn't indicate if the Abyss remains open for the whole five months or not while the locusts inflict their stings on those who do not have the mark of God on their foreheads, but it does say that the plague of locusts lasts for five months. But regardless, with all this darkness to look forward to, the world's oil will certainly be a much sought-after commodity, for it will be in high demand in order to power all the electric lighting that will be needed so that people can see what they are doing in the darkness. I know—I don't really want to be here then either! But if we're still alive, we will be, so it might

---

[87] See (http://aa.usno.navy.mil/data/docs/Dur_OneYear.php) to determine the length of daylight hours in your area during a particular day of the year—*if* you want to do your own calculations.

be a good idea to have lots of flashlights and batteries on hand.

After experiencing both the fourth and fifth trumpet plagues of Revelation, by the time the celestial events of the *day of the Lord* begin impacting the earth, it should certainly get the world's attention! At that time, the sign of the Son of Man, shining in all his resplendent heavenly brightness and glory, will be a stark contrast, indeed, compared to all the darkness that will have become so prevalent to those living on the earth. The whole world will definitely see the "sign of the Son of Man" appearing in the heavens and the Bible says that the whole earth will mourn because of him!

Time is passing, and the days are slowly ticking away like seconds on a clock, until the time will finally arrive—when it will absolutely be—the *last day*. Be blessed! Thanks for reading this book.

# Appendices

Appendices

# Appendix A

# Merged Gospel Narrative
## Olivet Discourse
*Matthew 24:1-51; Mark 13:1-35; Luke 21:5-36*

## *(Without Comments)*

## *1*
## *The Temple Prophecies*

[Mt 24:1] Jesus left the temple and was walking away when his disciples came up to him to call his attention to its buildings. [Mk 13:1] As Jesus was leaving the temple, one of his disciples said to him, "Look, Teacher! What massive stones! What magnificent buildings!" [Lk 21:5] Some of his disciples were remarking about how the temple was adorned with beautiful stones and with gifts dedicated to God. But Jesus said, [Mt 24:2] "Do you see all these things?" he asked. "Truly I tell you, not one stone here will be left on another; every one will be thrown down." [Mk 13:2] "Do you see all these great buildings?" replied Jesus. "Not one stone here will be left on another; every one will be thrown down." [Lk 21:6] "As for what you see here, the time will come when not one stone will be left on another; every one of them will be thrown down."

# 2
# *The Disciples' Four Questions*

[Mt 24:3] As Jesus was sitting on the Mount of Olives, the disciples came to him privately. "Tell us," they said, "when will this happen, and what will be the sign of your coming and of the end of the age?" [Mk 13:3] As Jesus was sitting on the Mount of Olives opposite the temple, Peter, James, John and Andrew asked him privately, [4] "Tell us, when will these things happen? And what will be the sign that they are all about to be fulfilled?" [Lk 21:8] "Teacher," they asked, "when will these things happen? And what will be the sign that they are about to take place?"

# 3
# *Beginning of Birth Pains*

[Mt 24:4-7] Jesus answered: "Watch out that no one deceives you. [5] For many will come in my name, claiming, 'I am the Messiah,' and will deceive many. [6] You will hear of wars and rumors of wars, but see to it that you are not alarmed. Such things must happen, but the end is still to come. [7] Nation will rise against nation, and kingdom against kingdom. There will be famines and earthquakes in various places. [8] All these are the beginning of birth pains." [Mk 13:5-8] Jesus said to them: "Watch out that no one deceives you. [6] Many will come in my name, claiming, 'I am he,' and will deceive many. [7] When you hear of wars and rumors of wars, do not be alarmed. Such things must happen, but the end is still to come. [8] Nation will rise against nation, and kingdom against kingdom. There will be earthquakes in various places, and famines. These are the beginning of birth pains." [Lk 21:8-11] He replied: "Watch out that you are not deceived. For many will come in my name, claiming, 'I am he,' and, 'The time is near.' Do not follow them. [9] When you hear of wars and uprisings, do not be frightened. These things must happen first, but the end will not come right away." [10] Then he said to them: "Nation will rise against nation, and kingdom against kingdom. [11] There will be great earthquakes, famines and pestilences in various places, and fearful events and great signs from heaven."

# *4*

# *Personal Prophesies to the Disciples*
*"Before all this, they will seize you and persecute you."*

[Lk 21:12-18] *But before all this*, they will seize you and persecute you. They will hand you over to synagogues and put you in prison, and you will be brought before kings and governors, and all on account of my name. [13] And so you will bear testimony to me. [14] But make up your mind not to worry beforehand how you will defend yourselves. [15] For I will give you words and wisdom that none of your adversaries will be able to resist or contradict. [16] You will be betrayed even by parents, brothers and sisters, relatives and friends, and they will put some of you to death. [17] Everyone will hate you because of me. [18] But not a hair of your head will perish. [19] Stand firm, and you will win life. **[Mt 24:9-14]** Then you will be handed over to be persecuted and put to death, and you will be hated by all nations because of me. [10] At that time many will turn away from the faith and will betray and hate each other, [11] and many false prophets will appear and deceive many people. [12] Because of the increase of wickedness, the love of most will grow cold, [13] but the one who stands firm to the end will be saved. [14] And this gospel of the kingdom will be preached in the whole world as a testimony to all nations, and then the end will come. **[Mk 13:9-13]** You must be on your guard. You will be handed over to the local councils and flogged in the synagogues. On account of me you will stand before governors and kings as witnesses to them. [10] And the gospel must first be preached to all nations. [11] Whenever you are arrested and brought to trial, do not worry beforehand about what to say. Just say whatever is given you at the time, for it is not you speaking, but the Holy Spirit. [12] Brother will betray brother to death, and a father his child. Children will rebel against their parents and have them put to death. [13] Everyone will hate you because of me, but the one who stands firm to the end will be saved.

# 5
# *Abomination that causes Desolation*
"Then let those who are in Judea
Flee to the mountains"
"There will be great distress in the land"
and wrath against this people"

[Mt 24:15-28] So when you see standing in the holy place "the abomination that causes desolation," spoken of through the prophet Daniel—let the reader understand— [16] then let those who are in Judea flee to the mountains. [17] Let no one on the housetop go down to take anything out of the house. [18] Let no one in the field go back to get their cloak. [19] How dreadful it will be in those days for pregnant women and nursing mothers! [20] Pray that your flight will not take place in winter or on the Sabbath. [21] For then there will be great distress, unequaled from the beginning of the world until now—and never to be equaled again. [22] If those days had not been cut short, no one would survive, but for the sake of the elect those days will be shortened. [23] At that time if anyone says to you, "Look, here is the Messiah!" or, "There he is!" do not believe it. [24] For false messiahs and false prophets will appear and perform great signs and wonders to deceive, if possible, even the elect. [25] See, I have told you ahead of time. [26] So if anyone tells you, "There he is, out in the wilderness," do not go out; or, "Here he is, in the inner rooms," do not believe it. [27] For as lightning that comes from the east is visible even in the west, so will be the coming of the Son of Man. [28] Wherever there is a carcass, there the vultures will gather. [Mk 13:14-23] When you see "the abomination that causes desolation" standing where it does not belong—let the reader understand—then let those who are in Judea flee to the mountains. [15] Let no one on the housetop go down or enter the house to take anything out. [16] Let no one in the field go back to get their cloak. [17] How dreadful it will be in those days for pregnant women and nursing mothers! [18] Pray that this will not take place in winter, [19] because those will be days of distress unequaled from the beginning, when God created the world, until now—and never to be equaled again. [20] If the Lord had not cut short those days, no one would survive. But for the sake of the elect, whom he has chosen, he has shortened them. [21] At that time if anyone says to you, "Look, here is the Messiah!" or, "Look, there he is!" do not believe it. [22] For false messiahs and false prophets will appear and perform signs and wonders to deceive, if possible, even the elect. [23] So be on your guard; I have told you everything ahead of time. [Lk 21:20-24] When you see Jerusalem being surrounded by armies, you will know that its desolation is near. [21] Then let those who are in Judea flee to the mountains, let those in the city get out, and let those in the country not enter the city.

[22] For this is the time of punishment in fulfillment of all that has been written. [23] How dreadful it will be in those days for pregnant women and nursing mothers! There will be great distress in the land and wrath against this people. [24] They will fall by the sword and will be taken as prisoners to all the nations. Jerusalem will be trampled on by the Gentiles until the times of the Gentiles are fulfilled.

# 6

## *The Day of the Lord*
### *"Immediately after the distress of those days"*

[Mt 24:29-31] Immediately after the distress of those days "the sun will be darkened, and the moon will not give its light; the stars will fall from the sky, and the heavenly bodies will be shaken." [30] Then will appear the sign of the Son of Man in heaven. And then all the peoples of the earth will mourn when they see the Son of Man coming on the clouds of heaven, with power and great glory. [31] And he will send his angels with a loud trumpet call, and they will gather his elect from the four winds, from one end of the heavens to the other. [Mk 13:24-27] But in those days, following that distress, "the sun will be darkened, and the moon will not give its light; [25] the stars will fall from the sky, and the heavenly bodies will be shaken." [26] At that time people will see the Son of Man coming in clouds with great power and glory. [27] And he will send his angels and gather his elect from the four winds, from the ends of the earth to the ends of the heavens. **[Lk21:25-28]** There will be signs in the sun, moon and stars. On the earth, nations will be in anguish and perplexity at the roaring and tossing of the sea. [26] People will faint from terror, apprehensive of what is coming on the world, for the heavenly bodies will be shaken. [27] At that time they will see the Son of Man coming in a cloud with power and great glory. [28] When these things begin to take place, stand up and lift up your heads, because your redemption is drawing near.

# 7

## *Lesson of the Fig Tree and All Trees*
*"When you see these things happening,
you know that the kingdom of God is near"*

**[Mt 24:32-35]** Now learn this lesson from the fig tree: As soon as its twigs get tender and its leaves come out, you know that summer is near. [33] Even so, when you see all these things, you know that it is near, right at the door. [34] Truly I tell you, this generation will certainly not pass away until all these things have happened. [35] Heaven and earth will pass away, but my words will never pass away. **[Mk 13:28-31]** Now learn this lesson from the fig tree: As soon as its twigs get tender and its leaves come out, you know that summer is near. [29] Even so, when you see these things happening, you know that it is near, right at the door. [30] Truly I tell you, this generation will certainly not pass away until all these things have happened. [31] Heaven and earth will pass away, but my words will never pass away. [Lk 21:29-33] He told them this parable: "Look at the fig tree and all the trees. [30] When they sprout leaves, you can see for yourselves and know that summer is near. [31] Even so, when you see these things happening, you know that the kingdom of God is near. [32] "Truly I tell you, this generation will certainly not pass away until all these things have happened. [33] Heaven and earth will pass away, but my words will never pass away."

# 8

## *The Unknown Day and Hour*

*"Therefore keep watch, because you do not know on what day your Lord will come"*

[Mt 24:36-44] "But about that day or hour no one knows, not even the angels in heaven, nor the Son, but only the Father. [37] As it was in the days of Noah, so it will be at the coming of the Son of Man. [38] For in the days before the flood, people were eating and drinking, marrying and giving in marriage, up to the day Noah entered the ark; [39] and they knew nothing about what would happen until the flood came and took them all away. That is how it will be at the coming of the Son of Man. [40] Two men will be in the field; one will be taken and the other left. [41] Two women will be grinding with a hand mill; one will be taken and the other left. [42] Therefore keep watch, because you do not know on what day your Lord will come. [43] But understand this: If the owner of the house had known at what time of night the thief was coming, he would have kept watch and would not have let his house be broken into. [44] So you also must be ready, because the Son of Man will come at an hour when you do not expect him. [Mk 13:32-37] But about that day or hour no one knows, not even the angels in heaven, nor the Son, but only the Father. [33] Be on guard! Be alert! You do not know when that time will come. [34] It's like a man going away: He leaves his house and puts his servants in charge, each with their assigned task, and tells the one at the door to keep watch. [35] Therefore keep watch because you do not know when the owner of the house will come back—whether in the evening, or at midnight, or when the rooster crows, or at dawn. [36] If he comes suddenly, do not let him find you sleeping. [37] What I say to you, I say to everyone: 'Watch!' [Lk 21:34-36] Be careful, or your hearts will be weighed down with carousing, drunkenness and the anxieties of life, and that day will close on you suddenly like a trap. [35] For it will come on all those who live on the face of the whole earth. [36] Be always on the watch, and pray that you may be able to escape all that is about to happen, and that you may be able to stand before the Son of Man." [Lk 17:22-37] "Then he said to his disciples, 'The time is coming when you will long to see one of the days of the Son of Man, but you will not see it. [23] Men will tell you, 'There he is!' or 'Here he is!' Do not go running off after them. [24] For the Son of Man in his day will be like the lightning, which flashes and lights up the sky from one end to the other. [25] But first he must suffer many things and be rejected by this generation. [26] Just as it was in the days of Noah, so also will it be in the days of the Son of Man. [27] People were eating, drinking, marrying and being given in marriage up to the day Noah entered the ark. Then the flood came and destroyed them all. [28] It was the same in the days of Lot. People were eating and drinking, buying and selling, planting and building. [29] But the day Lot left Sodom, fire and sulfur rained down from heaven and destroyed them all. [30] It will be just like this on the day the Son of Man is revealed. [31] On that day no one who is on the roof of his house, with his goods inside, should go down to get them. Likewise, no one in the field should go back for anything. [32] Remember Lot's wife! [33] Whoever tries to keep his life will lose it, and whoever loses his life will preserve it. [34] I tell you, on that night two people will be in one bed; one will be taken and the other left. [35] Two women will be grinding grain together; one will be taken and the other left.' [37] 'Where, Lord?' they asked. He replied, 'Where there is a dead body, there the vultures will gather.'"

# 9
# *Faithful and Wise Servant Parable*

[Mt 24:45-51] Who then is the faithful and wise servant, whom the master has put in charge of the servants in his household to give them their food at the proper time? [46] It will be good for that servant whose master finds him doing so when he returns. [47] Truly I tell you, he will put him in charge of all his possessions. [48] But suppose that servant is wicked and says to himself, "My master is staying away a long time," [49] and he then begins to beat his fellow servants and to eat and drink with drunkards. [50] The master of that servant will come on a day when he does not expect him and at an hour he is not aware of. [51] He will cut him to pieces and assign him a place with the hypocrites, where there will be weeping and gnashing of teeth.

# *10*
## *Ten Virgins Parable*

[Mt 25:1-13] At that time the kingdom of heaven will be like ten virgins who took their lamps and went out to meet the bridegroom. [2] Five of them were foolish and five were wise. [3] The foolish ones took their lamps but did not take any oil with them. [4] The wise ones, however, took oil in jars along with their lamps. [5] The bridegroom was a long time in coming, and they all became drowsy and fell asleep. [6] At midnight the cry rang out: "Here's the bridegroom! Come out to meet him!" [7] Then all the virgins woke up and trimmed their lamps. [8] The foolish ones said to the wise, "Give us some of your oil; our lamps are going out." [9] "No," they replied, "there may not be enough for both us and you. Instead, go to those who sell oil and buy some for yourselves." [10] But while they were on their way to buy the oil, the bridegroom arrived. The virgins who were ready went in with him to the wedding banquet. And the door was shut. [11] Later the others also came. "Lord, Lord," they said, "open the door for us!" [12] But he replied, "Truly I tell you, I don't know you." [13] Therefore keep watch, because you do not know the day or the hour.

# 11
## *Bags of Gold Parable*

[Mt 25:14-18] Again, it will be like a man going on a journey, who called his servants and entrusted his wealth to them. [15] To one he gave five bags of gold, to another two bags, and to another one bag, each according to his ability. Then he went on his journey. [16] The man who had received five bags of gold went at once and put his money to work and gained five bags more. [17] So also, the one with two bags of gold gained two more. [18] But the man who had received one bag went off, dug a hole in the ground and hid his master's money.

[Mt 25:19-21] After a long time the master of those servants returned and settled accounts with them. [20] The man who had received five bags of gold brought the other five. "Master," he said, "you entrusted me with five bags of gold. See, I have gained five more." [21] His master replied, "Well done, good and faithful servant! You have been faithful with a few things; I will put you in charge of many things. Come and share your master's happiness!" [Mt 25:22-23] The man with two bags of gold also came. "Master," he said, "you entrusted me with two bags of gold; see, I have gained two more." [23] His master replied, "Well done, good and faithful servant! You have been faithful with a few things; I will put you in charge of many things. Come and share your master's happiness!"

[Mt 25:24-30] Then the man who had received one bag of gold came. "Master," he said, "I knew that you are a hard man, harvesting where you have not sown and gathering where you have not scattered seed. [25] So I was afraid and went out and hid your gold in the ground. See, here is what belongs to you." [26] His master replied, "You wicked, lazy servant! So you knew that I harvest where I have not sown and gather where I have not scattered seed? [27] Well then, you should have put my money on deposit with the bankers, so that when I returned I would have received it back with interest. [28] So take the bag of gold from him and give it to the one who has ten bags. [29] For whoever has will be given more, and they will have an abundance. Whoever does not have, even what they have will be taken from them. [30] And throw that worthless servant outside, into the darkness, where there will be weeping and gnashing of teeth."

# 12
## *Sheep and Goats Parable*

[Mt 25:31-40] When the Son of Man comes in his glory, and all the angels with him, he will sit on his glorious throne. [32] All the nations will be gathered before him, and he will separate the people one from another as a shepherd separates the sheep from the goats. [33] He will put the sheep on his right and the goats on his left. [34] Then the King will say to those on his right, "Come, you who are blessed by my Father; take your inheritance, the kingdom prepared for you since the creation of the world. [35] For I was hungry and you gave me something to eat, I was thirsty and you gave me something to drink, I was a stranger and you invited me in, [36] I needed clothes and you clothed me, I was sick and you looked after me, I was in prison and you came to visit me." [37] Then the righteous will answer him, "Lord, when did we see you hungry and feed you, or thirsty and give you something to drink? [38] When did we see you a stranger and invite you in, or needing clothes and clothe you? [39] When did we see you sick or in prison and go to visit you?" [40] The King will reply, "Truly I tell you, whatever you did for one of the least of these brothers and sisters of mine, you did for me."

[Mt 25:41-46] Then he will say to those on his left, "Depart from me, you who are cursed, into the eternal fire prepared for the devil and his angels. [42] For I was hungry and you gave me nothing to eat, I was thirsty and you gave me nothing to drink, [43] I was a stranger and you did not invite me in, I needed clothes and you did not clothe me, I was sick and in prison and you did not look after me." [44] They also will answer, "Lord, when did we see you hungry or thirsty or a stranger or needing clothes or sick or in prison, and did not help you?" [45] He will reply, "Truly I tell you, whatever you did not do for one of the least of these, you did not do for me." [46] Then they will go away to eternal punishment, but the righteous to eternal life.

# Appendix B

# Scriptures on The Rapture

## *From the Old and New Testaments*
(All scriptures from the NIV unless otherwise noted)

### *Isaiah 26:19*
But your dead will live, Lord;
their bodies will rise—
let those who dwell in the dust
wake up and shout for joy—
your dew is like the dew of the morning;
the earth will give birth to her dead.

### *Daniel 12:2*
Multitudes who sleep in the dust of the earth will awake:
some to everlasting life, others to shame and everlasting
contempt.

### *Matthew 24:30-31*
Then will appear the sign of the Son of Man in heaven. And
then all the peoples of the earth will mourn when they see the
Son of Man coming on the clouds of heaven, with power and
great glory. [31] And he will send his angels with a loud trumpet
call, and they will gather his elect from the four winds, from
one end of the heavens to the other.

### *Matthew 25:1-13*

At that time the kingdom of heaven will be like ten virgins who took their lamps and went out to meet the bridegroom. ² Five of them were foolish and five were wise. ³ The foolish ones took their lamps but did not take any oil with them. ⁴ The wise ones, however, took oil in jars along with their lamps. ⁵ The bridegroom was a long time in coming, and they all became drowsy and fell asleep. ⁶ At midnight the cry rang out: "Here's the bridegroom! Come out to meet him!" ⁷ Then all the virgins woke up and trimmed their lamps. ⁸ The foolish ones said to the wise, "Give us some of your oil; our lamps are going out." ⁹ "No," they replied, "there may not be enough for both us and you. Instead, go to those who sell oil and buy some for yourselves." ¹⁰ But while they were on their way to buy the oil, the bridegroom arrived. The virgins who were ready went in with him to the wedding banquet. And the door was shut. ¹¹Later the others also came. "Lord, Lord," they said, "open the door for us!" ¹² "But he replied, "Truly I tell you, I don't know you." ¹³ Therefore keep watch, because you do not know the day or the hour.

### *Mark 13:24-27*

But in those days, following that distress, "the sun will be darkened, and the moon will not give its light; ²⁵ the stars will fall from the sky, and the heavenly bodies will be shaken." ²⁶ At that time people will see the Son of Man coming in clouds with great power and glory. ²⁷ And he will send his angels and gather his elect from the four winds, from the ends of the earth to the ends of the heavens.

### Luke 17:30-35

It will be just like this on the day the Son of Man is revealed. [31] On that day no one who is on the housetop, with possessions inside, should go down to get them. Likewise, no one in the field should go back for anything. [32] Remember Lot's wife! [33] Whoever tries to keep their life will lose it, and whoever loses their life will preserve it. [34] I tell you, on that night two people will be in one bed; one will be taken and the other left. [35] Two women will be grinding grain together; one will be taken and the other left.

### Luke 21:25-28

There will be signs in the sun, moon and stars. On the earth, nations will be in anguish and perplexity at the roaring and tossing of the sea. [26] People will faint from terror, apprehensive of what is coming on the world, for the heavenly bodies will be shaken. [27] At that time they will see the Son of Man coming in a cloud with power and great glory. [28] When these things begin to take place, stand up and lift up your heads, because your redemption is drawing near.

### Luke 21:34-36

Be careful, or your hearts will be weighed down with carousing, drunkenness and the anxieties of life, and that day will close on you suddenly like a trap. [35] For it will come on all those who live on the face of the whole earth. [36] Be always on the watch, and pray that you may be able to escape all that is about to happen, and that you may be able to stand before the Son of Man.

*Appendix B*

### John 6:39-40
And this is the will of him who sent me, that I shall lose none
of all those he has given me, but raise them up at the last day.
[40] For my Father's will is that everyone who looks to the Son
and believes in him shall have eternal life, and I will raise them
up at the last day.

### John 6:44
No one can come to me unless the Father who sent me draws
them, and I will raise them up at the last day.

### John 6:54
Whoever eats my flesh and drinks my blood has eternal life,
and I will raise them up at the last day.

### John 11:24
Martha answered, "I know he will rise again in the
resurrection at the last day.

### 1 Corinthians 15:51-52
Listen, I tell you a mystery: We will not all sleep, but we will all
be changed— [52] in a flash, in the twinkling of an eye, at the
last trumpet. For the trumpet will sound, the dead will be
raised imperishable, and we will be changed.

### 2 Thessalonians 1:6-10
God is just: He will pay back trouble to those who trouble you
[7] and give relief to you who are troubled, and to us as well.
This will happen when the Lord Jesus is revealed from heaven
in blazing fire with his powerful angels. [8] He will punish those
who do not know God and do not obey the gospel of our Lord
Jesus. [9] They will be punished with everlasting destruction and

shut out from the presence of the Lord and from the glory of his might [10] on the day he comes to be glorified in his holy people and to be marveled at among all those who have believed. This includes you, because you believed our testimony to you.

### 2 Thessalonians 2:1-12

Concerning the coming of our Lord Jesus Christ and our being gathered to him, we ask you, brothers and sisters, [2] not to become easily unsettled or alarmed by the teaching allegedly from us—whether by a prophecy or by word of mouth or by letter—asserting that the day of the Lord has already come. [3] Don't let anyone deceive you in any way, for that day will not come until the rebellion occurs and the man of lawlessness is revealed, the man doomed to destruction. [4] He will oppose and will exalt himself over everything that is called God or is worshiped, so that he sets himself up in God's temple, proclaiming himself to be God.

[5] Don't you remember that when I was with you I used to tell you these things? [6] And now you know what is holding him back, so that he may be revealed at the proper time. [7] For the secret power of lawlessness is already at work; but the one who now holds it back will continue to do so till he is taken out of the way. [8] And then the lawless one will be revealed, whom the Lord Jesus will overthrow with the breath of his mouth and destroy by the splendor of his coming. [9] The coming of the lawless one will be in accordance with how Satan works. He will use all sorts of displays of power through signs and wonders that serve the lie, [10] and all the ways that wickedness deceives those who are perishing. They perish

because they refused to love the truth and so be saved. [88]For this reason God sends them a powerful delusion so that they will believe the lie and so that all will be condemned who have not believed the truth but have delighted in wickedness.

### Titus 2:13-14
while we wait for the blessed hope—the appearing of the glory of our great God and Savior, Jesus Christ, who gave himself for us to redeem us from all wickedness and to purify for himself a people that are his very own, eager to do what is good.

### Hebrews 9:28
So Christ was sacrificed once to take away the sins of many; and he will appear a second time, not to bear sin, but to bring salvation to those who are waiting for him.

### 1 Peter 5:4
And when the Chief Shepherd appears, you will receive the crown of glory that will never fade away.

### 1 John 3:2
Dear friends, now we are children of God, and what we will be has not yet been made known. But we know that when Christ appears, we shall be like him, for we shall see him as he is.

### Revelation 3:3
Remember, therefore, what you have received and heard; hold it fast, and repent. But if you do not wake up, I will come

---

[88] Vs 11-12

like a thief, and you will not know at what time I will come to you.

**Revelation 3:10**
Since you have kept my command to endure patiently, I will also keep you from the hour of trial that is going to come on the whole world to test the inhabitants of the earth.

**Revelation 10:7**
[89]But in the days of the voice of the seventh angel, when he shall begin to sound the trumpet, the mystery of God shall be finished, as he hath declared by his servants the prophets.

**Revelation 16:15**
Look, I come like a thief! Blessed is the one who stays awake and remains clothed, so as not to go naked and be shamefully exposed.

---

[89] Douay-Rheims 1899 American Edition

## Appendix C

## Merged Gospel Narrative

# Sequences of Events

## *Plus Daniel Chapter 9 Sequence*

*Jesus' Teachings on End Times*
*From Matthew, Mark and Luke*

### *Personal Prophesies to the Disciples*

#### *(Part 4, Chapter 2)*

*Plight of the Early Church Jews*
**[Mt 24:9-14] [Mk 13:9-13] [Lk 21:12-18]**

1. They will seize you and persecute you.
2. They will hand you over to synagogues and put you in prison.
3. You will be brought before kings and governors.
4. You will bear testimony to me.
5. I will give you words and wisdom that none of your adversaries will be able to resist or contradict.
6. You will be betrayed.
7. They will put some of you to death.
8. Everyone will hate you because of me.
9. Many will turn away from the faith and will betray and hate each other.
10. Many false prophets will appear and deceive many people.

## *Beginning of Birth Pains*
### *(Part 3, Chapter 2)*
#### [Mt 24:4-7] [Mk 13:5-8] [Lk21:8-11]

11. False messiahs appear and will deceive many.

12. Wars and rumors of wars.

13. Nation will rise against nation, and kingdom against kingdom.

14. There will be earthquakes, famines and pestilences in various places.

15. There will be fearful events and great signs from heaven.

## *Abomination that Causes Desolation*
### *(Part 5, Chapter 2)*
#### *Plight of the Modern Day Jews*
#### [Mt 24:15-28] [Mk 13:14-23] [Lk 21:20-24]

16. Jerusalem will be surrounded by armies just before its desolation is near.  For this is the time of punishment in fulfillment of all that has been written.

17. The abomination that causes desolation will be seen standing in the holy place.

18. Then there will be great distress in the land and wrath against this [the Jewish] people.

19. "At that time...false messiahs and false prophets will appear and perform great signs and wonders to deceive..."
20. They [the Jews] will fall by the sword and will be taken as prisoners to all the nations.
21. Jerusalem will be trampled on by the Gentiles until the times of the Gentiles are fulfilled.

## *The Day of the Lord*
### *(Part 6, Chapter 2)*
[Mt 24:29-31] [Mk 13:24-27] [Lk21:25-28]

22. Immediately after the distress of those days, the sun will be darkened, and the moon will not give its light.
23. The stars will fall from the sky, and the heavenly bodies will be shaken.
24. Nations will be in anguish and perplexity at the roaring and tossing of the sea. People will faint from terror, apprehensive of what is coming on the world.
25. Then will appear the sign of the Son of Man in heaven.
26. All the peoples of the earth will mourn when they see the Son of Man coming on the clouds of heaven, with power and great glory.

27. He will send his angels with a loud trumpet call,
    and they will gather his elect from the four winds,
    from one end of the heavens to the other.

# Daniel Chapter 9

## Sequence of Events
### [Daniel 9:25-27]

1.  The word goes out to restore and rebuild
    Jerusalem.
2.  It is rebuilt with streets and a trench, but in times
    of trouble.
3.  Seven sevens and sixty-two sevens of time pass (49
    + 434 = 483 years).
4.  The Anointed One is put to death and has nothing.
5.  The people of the ruler who will come destroy the
    city [Jerusalem] and the sanctuary. [Temple
    destruction prophecy of Jesus is fulfilled]
6.  War continues, and desolations are decreed.
7.  He [the ruler who will come] confirms [or
    strengthens] a covenant with many for one 'seven.'
8.  In the middle of the 'seven' he puts an end to
    sacrifice and offering (3 ½ years, 1260 days).  He
    [the ruler who will come] sets up an abomination
    that causes desolation at the temple.
9.  The end comes like a flood—the end that is
    decreed is poured out on him [the ruler who will
    come].

# Revelation 10:7
## *Interpretation*

The New International Version translates Revelation 10:7 as follows: "But in the days when the seventh angel is *about* to sound his trumpet, the mystery of God will be accomplished, just as he announced to his servants the prophets." The Douay-Rheims 1899 American Edition translates it like this: "But in the days of the voice of the seventh angel, when he shall *begin* to sound the trumpet, the mystery of God shall be finished, as he hath declared by his servants the prophets."

Whether the seventh angel is *about* to sound, or whether he *begins* to sound his trumpet, the time element is so close here that it really doesn't matter as far as *when* the mystery of God takes place. What does matter is the purpose of this passage of scripture, and how it relates to the mystery of God contained therein.

First of all, there are three essential elements that are connected to this Revelation 10:7 passage: they are (1) the seventh or last trumpet of Revelation being sounded or being about to sound, (2) the mystery of God being accomplished either before or during the blast of the seventh trumpet, and (3) the fact that this mystery of God was spoken through God's servants the prophets. Also just as important here is the context of the Revelation 10:1-7 passage within which this scripture is contained; so that if we allow ourselves to be guided by scripture's contents and context, then the scripture itself should designate how verse seven of this particular Revelation passage should be interpreted.

Please realize, that *If* there are *NO* mysteries of God to be found in the Bible that are associated with a seventh or last trumpet, then we, from this passage alone, cannot really know which mystery of God this passage would be referencing—we could only speculate.

However, since the Bible *does* contain a mystery of God associated with a last trumpet, 1 Corinthians 15:51-52, then we should investigate it, along with any scriptures that are related to it, in order to see if all these scriptures, when considered together, will be found harmonious—that is, whether or not they will demonstrate compatibility. If they do, then we should next examine the context within which this scripture verse is found to determine if the context for this verse matches the contexts of the other related verses. If so, then as long as this particular mystery of God was foretold by God's servants the prophets, which is a qualifier found in Revelation 10:7, then we will know for certain whether the mystery of God will be accomplished *before* or *during* the blast of the seventh trumpet of Revelation.

Since there is a mystery of God associated with a last trumpet, let's give this mystery consideration. The only mystery of God associated with a last trumpet was written by the Apostle Paul, and it is found in 1 Corinthians 15:51-52 where it says, "Listen, I tell you a mystery: We will not all sleep, but we will all be changed— in a flash, in the twinkling of an eye, at the last trumpet. For the trumpet will sound, the dead will be raised imperishable, and we will be changed."

The Apostle Paul says here that it happens "... *at* the last trumpet." He does not say it will happen before the last trumpet. The word "at" in this case could mean that it will occur when the last trumpet *begins* to sound, or *during* the sounding of the last trumpet. Jesus also said in Matthew 24:31 that he will "send his angels *with* a loud trumpet call, and they will gather his elect from the four winds, from one end of the heavens to the other." The word "with" in this case certainly means during the sounding of the trumpet since the trumpet call is what actually signals the angels into action. So these verses would indicate that when the trumpet has begun to sound, or while it is sounding, the corresponding actions will take place.

The Apostle Paul then ties everything together in 1 Thessalonians 4:16 where he says, "For the Lord himself will come down from heaven, *with* a [90]loud command, *with* the voice of the archangel, and *with* the trumpet call of God, and

---

[90] Greek word, "Keleuma" Strongs no. 1752: It means an order, command, spec. a stimulating cry, either that by which animals are roused and urged on by man, as horses by charioteers, hounds by hunters, etc., or that by which a signal is given to men, e.g. to rowers by the master of a ship, to soldiers by a commander (with a loud summons, a trumpet call). From the Greek lexicon based on Thayer's and Smith's Bible Dictionary plus others; this is keyed to the large Kittel and the "Theological Dictionary of the New Testament." These files are public domain.

the dead in Christ will rise first.  After that, we who are still alive and are left will be caught up together with them in the clouds to meet the Lord in the air..."

So according to the Apostle Paul, three things occur in a timed sequence during the time the Lord himself also descends from heaven to Earth's atmosphere: he descends *with* a loud command, *with* the voice of the archangel, and *with* the trumpet call of God.  So during our Lord's descent: the loud command happens, the archangel's voice happens, and the trumpet call of God begins sounding, which signals and sends the angels gathering up his elect to meet the Lord in Earth's atmosphere; and all are transported by the angels to heaven. The Apostle Paul said that it would happen "in a flash, in the twinkling of an eye, at the last trumpet." We can see how the context of 1 Corinthians 15:51-52, Matthew 24:31, and 1 Thessalonians 4:16-17 all have to do with the gathering of the saints to meet the Lord in the air—the context is the same.

The context of Revelation 10:1-7 includes a mighty angel descending to the earth from heaven, who gives a loud cry like the roar of a lion, then prophesies, "There will be no more delay! But in the days when the seventh angel begins to sound his trumpet, the mystery of God will be accomplished, just as he announced to his servants the prophets."

Afterward, the verses of Revelation 10:8-11 through 11:1-14 are parenthetical, detailing events which occur after the sounding of the sixth trumpet, the second woe; so if we skip over these parenthetical passages, we are brought then to the final trumpet plague, the third woe—the sounding of the seventh and final trumpet—and this blast is carried out to its completion.

In heaven, *after* the sounding of the seventh trumpet, loud voices are heard saying: [91]"The kingdom of the world has become the kingdom of our Lord and of his Christ, and he will reign for ever and ever." This is when God takes his great power and begins to reign; for the nations were angry, and God's wrath has come. It is now the time for (1) judging the dead, and for (2) rewarding his servants the prophets, his saints, and those who reverence his name, AND, (3) for destroying those who destroy the earth.

On Earth, the seventh trumpet announces the last day, and the imminent beginning of the great and terrible day of the Lord—the day of vengeance—the time when God's wrath is poured out over the earth, for after the ark of God's covenant appears in the temple in heaven, the seven angels are given the seven bowls filled with the wrath of God.

So the blast of the seventh trumpet means salvation for those aligned with God, who have a relationship with him, but it means God's wrath has come to the inhabitants who still remain on the earth.

The seventh angel surely understands the significance of what is about to happen as he prepares himself to sound the seventh and final trumpet—there is an imminence and expectancy that develops in the angel's heart at that very

---

[91] Revelation 11:15-19;Revelation 15:5-8;16:1-21

moment when he is commanded to sound his shofar, and it is at that split second when the angel engages wholeheartedly to carry out his act to its completion, that the mystery of God is accomplished—in a flash, in the twinkling of an eye—at the last trumpet!

Think of Abraham—when he was on Mount Moriah, ready to sacrifice his only son, Isaac, to the Lord in obedience to what God had commanded him to do; Genesis 22:10 says, "he reached out his hand and took the knife to slay his son." It wasn't until that very moment when Abraham had determined in his heart to take the knife and to slay his son that the angel of God stopped him. For with God, *the heart point is the start point* of any action of obedience or disobedience. Jesus also makes this very clear in Matthew 5:28, where he said, "But I tell you that anyone who looks at a woman lustfully has already committed adultery with her in his heart. Again, *the heart point is the start point* with God.

So, to properly interpret the timing of when "the mystery of God will be accomplished, just as he announced to his servants the prophets," it will occur at that moment when the seventh angel determines in his heart and actually initiates the blast; so as the seventh angel *begins* to sound his trumpet, but before the sound has ended, "the mystery of God will be accomplished, just as he announced to his servants the prophets."

Remember, the seventh trumpet of Revelation is the *last* trumpet of Revelation; and that the ONLY *mystery of God* found in the Bible associated with a *last* trumpet is found in 1

154

Corinthians 15:51-52 where the Apostle Paul says, "Listen, I tell you a mystery: We will not all sleep, but we will all be changed—in a flash, in the twinkling of an eye, *at the last trumpet*. For the trumpet will sound, the dead will be raised imperishable, and we will be changed."  Don't forget, the Apostle Paul had the gift of prophecy.  Jesus was a prophet; and an Old Testament prophet who also prophesied about the resurrection part of the *rapture*, followed by God's wrath— was the Prophet Isaiah, who foretold about this event in Isaiah 26:19-21, where it says:

> "But your dead will live, Lord;
> their bodies will rise—
> let those who dwell in the dust
> wake up and shout for joy—
> your dew is like the dew of the morning;
> the earth will give birth to her dead.
>
> Go, my people, enter your rooms
> and shut the doors behind you;
> hide yourselves for a little while
> until his wrath has passed by.
>
> See, the Lord is coming out of his dwelling
> to punish the people of the earth for their sins.
> The earth will disclose the blood shed on it;
> the earth will conceal its slain no longer."

All three essential elements connected with the Revelation 10:7 passage are indeed compatible with the other related scriptures, and Jesus' as well as Paul's prophecies contribute and confirm that (1) when the seventh or last trumpet of Revelation begins sounding, (2) then the mystery of God will be accomplished, and (3) this mystery of God is, in fact, [92]"the coming of our Lord Jesus Christ and our being gathered to him" which was announced collectively through God's servants the prophets.

The first part of Revelation 10:7, where it reads in the Greek, "En ho hemera ho fonay ho hebdomos aggelos hoten mello salpizo...," could perhaps be rendered: "In that day which a tone that the seventh angel as soon as he intends to sound the trumpet..."

The Greek word *mello* indicates the imminence and certainty of the pending event's fulfillment once the will, the heart-decision of the angel, initiates the action of the blasting of the shofar in obedience to the command given him—the heart point being the start point of that action.

---

[92] 2 Thessalonians 2:1